A TASTE OF TUSCANY

To Doris at
Christmas,
1986

Love,

Dan

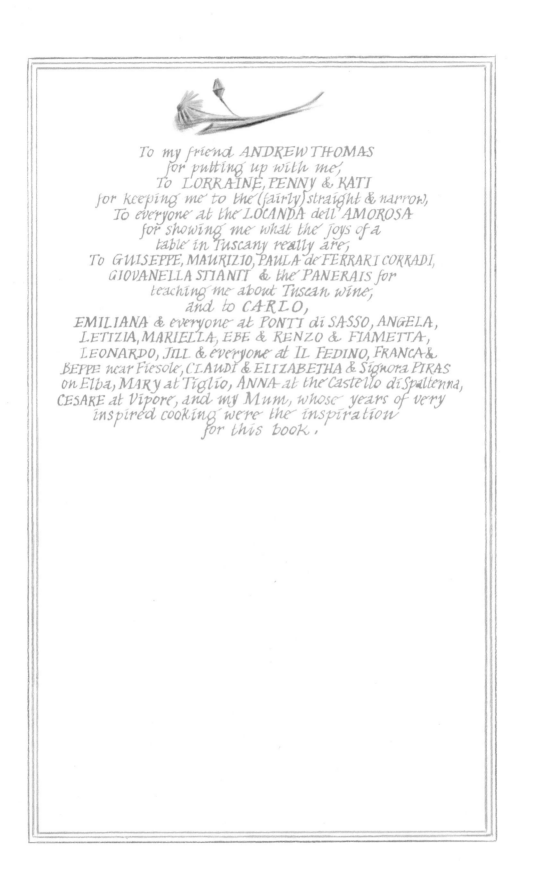

To my friend ANDREW THOMAS
for putting up with me;
To LORRAINE, PENNY & KATI
for keeping me to the (fairly) straight & narrow,
To everyone at the LOCANDA dell' AMOROSA
for showing me what the joys of a
table in Tuscany really are;
To GUISEPPE, MAURIZIO, PAULA de FERRARI CORRADI,
GIOVANELLA STIANTI & the PANERAIS for
teaching me about Tuscan wine;
and to CARLO,
EMILIANA & everyone at PONTI di SASSO, ANGELA,
LETIZIA, MARIELLA, EBE & RENZO & FIAMETTA,
LEONARDO, JILL & everyone at IL FEDINO, FRANCA &
BEPPE near Fiesole, CLAUDI & ELIZABETHA & Signora PIRAS
on Elba, MARY at Tiglio, ANNA at the Castello di Spaltenna,
CESARE at Vipore, and my Mum, whose years of very
inspired cooking were the inspiration
for this book.

A TASTE
OF TUSCANY

CLASSIC RECIPES
· from the ·
HEART of ITALY
COLLECTED and
ILLUSTRATED by
LESLIE FORBES

LITTLE, BROWN AND COMPANY
BOSTON ~ TORONTO

Library of Congress Catalog Card No. 85~50266
First American Edition

Produced by Johnson Editions Limited
30 Ingham Road, London NW6 1DE

Art editor Lorraine Johnson
Editor Penny Clarke

Printed and Bound in
Great Britain

· CONTENTS ·

· INTRODUCTION ·

A kitchen table on a farm near Mont Amiata, strewn with wild asparagus and giant porcini mushrooms, freshly gathered. A cafe table in Siena with slices of rich panforte and frothy cappucini for two. A table in a crowded Florentine trattoria, its checked cloth covered in plates of steaming spinach pasta. A pine table laden with pens, pencils and sketchpads in an olive grove north of Lucca. These are some of the many tables at which I ate, talked, drank and learned about Tuscany's culture and people as well her food and wine, and finally at which I distilled what I had learned into this book, more a sketchbook that grew than a traditional cookbook.

ASPARAGO

It started as a series of drawings and cooking notes on a trip to Tuscany five years ago. From that first trip my interest in the region developed over subsequent visits into a passion. I was hooked. For me Tuscany was, and still is, an irresistable combination of practical little family run restaurants casually serving up Italian sausages and beans next to grand Renaissance churches, of colourful food markets sprawling uninhibitedly across cobbled medieval piazzas and especially of people, some raucous and crafty, some gentle and reserved, all of them passionately and understandably proud of their region and its food & wine.

FUSILLI

BORAGINE

Tuscany was relatively poor until the recent onslaught of mass tourism, and as a result most of its cooking traditions are firmly rooted in what Italians call 'la cucina povera', the poor kitchen. A good Tuscan restaurant conforms to the principles of economical home cooking, using fresh local products rather than expensive imports. Chestnuts gathered from giant trees are used for sweet chestnut flour, the basis for many desserts. Pigs living outside for most of the year graze on

PENNE

FAGIOLI

6

SALVIA

AGLIO

the mast shed by the beech
trees, a fact that probably con~
tributes to the excellence of
Tuscan pork. Pine trees produce pine
nuts to bake in cakes and savouries. Everything
that can be used, is. Stale bread thickens soups
and stews, good leftover roast meat is served the
next day in a sauce of fresh herbs and succulent
plum tomatoes, extra pasta dough is baked with
sugar, rosemary and wine grapes to make
a rich juicy cake. And because of the
availability of wild mushrooms and
herbs, Tuscans eat food in their own
homes that many foreigners would
consider expensive luxuries.

PISELLI

TORTELLI

One of my fondest memories is of an
evening walk with a Flor~
entine friend in the hills above
Fiesole. Stopping to admire a tree~size ger~
anium outside a stone farmhouse, and to
chat with the proud owners, we were
rewarded with a jar of spicy tomato sauce
made by the farmer's wife and bouquets of
slender, just~gathered wild asparagus, as
rare, outside Tuscany, as orchids. In gen~
eral the best cooking is to be found like this,
in the home, or in restaurants well outside
central city areas. There is seldom a written menu
and this can lead to hilarious surprises, such as the
time I ordered what I thought was a light meal and
had instead a four hour, seven course eating mar~
athon with a climax of roast wild boar in a sauce of
pine nuts and bitter chocolate. Or the bowl of fish
soup called TEGAMACCIA, so full of bones and eel
spines that it was like eating a pincushion in
consommé. Such disasters are rare. Most Tuscan
dishes consist of colourful fresh ingredients
simply but imaginatively prepared with
local herbs like thyme, sage & rosemary.
It is a style of cooking with its
roots in the countryside
and in traditional
cooking methods basic~
ally unchanged since
the days of the Etruscans,

FUNGHI

FAVA

RAVIOLI

the ancient Italian tribe that first brought civil~
isation to Tuscany over 2000 years.

During the Renaissance, Tuscan cooking, like its art,
underwent a drastic change. This was the era when
one enthusiastic gourmet recommended stuffing a
wild boar with a goose, the goose with a pheasant, the
pheasant with a partridge, etc. on down the line to
finish with an olive. Florentine chefs took their skills
to barbaric France (where that very Italian device, the
fork, was still a rarity) and changed history. Recently
some of the dishes from those more exotic times have
been reintroduced by chefs anxious to bring more soph~
istication to Tuscan restaurants. But for me the best mom~
ents are still the simple & unsophisticated ones ~ those spent
learning from a cook the exact moment when eggs have
absorbed enough flour to give a firm but not tough pasta
dough. Or listening, in a tiny cramped Florentine trattoria,
while a chef describes how to make the perfect artichoke
omelette. Or sniffing the aroma of the chestnut cake 'cas~
tagnaccia' baking in a friend's kitchen, & burning my
fingers & tongue on deep~fried, sugary cenci, hot from a pan.

Each recipe in this book evokes a strong memory for me.
They were collected in extremely pleasant circumstances
from both professional & amateur cooks all over Tuscany.
Some are the inventions of individuals I met casually ~
like the dandelion soup made by a Montalcino grand~
mother or the recipe for hunter's sauce given by a travel~
ling porchetta vendor in San Gimignano.

Not all the recipes come word for word from the res~
taurants mentioned. Some I have had to adapt from
notes scribbled while a harassed chef continued to cook
the daily speciality. Most of the recipes can be adapted
to suit personal taste & some are just quick ideas for
giving a particularly Tuscan flavour to a standard recipe,
such as the rosemary~flavoured oil that, added to basic
bread dough, instantly conjures up a steamy Florence
bakeshop at Easter.

I hope that, when cooked in some distant kitchen,
these recipes will bring at least a few of the pleas~
ures of a table in Tuscany. And that everyone who
shares my nostalgia for such pleasures will find some~
thing in this book to stir fond memories.

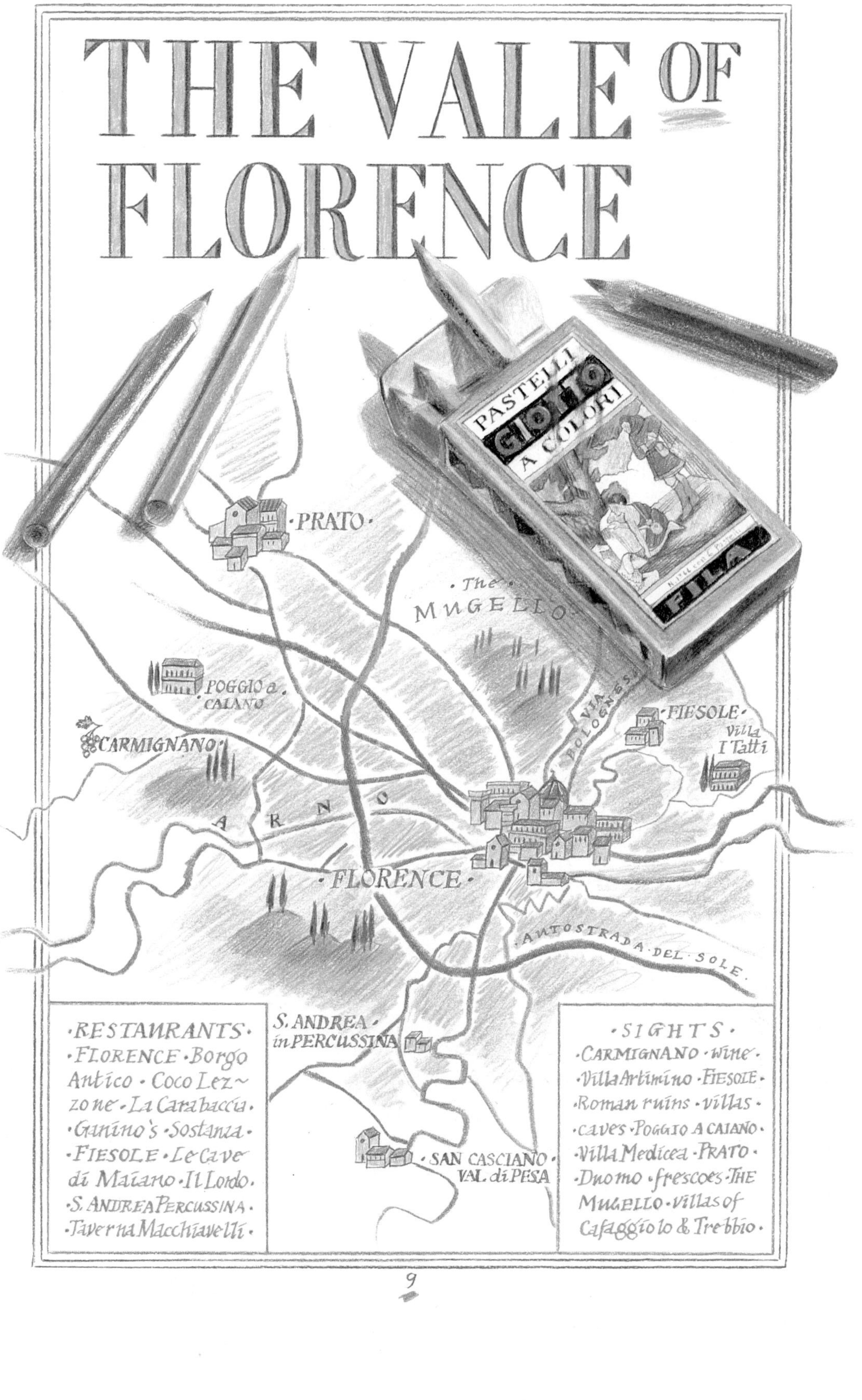
THE VALE OF FLORENCE
PASTELLI
GIOTTO
A COLORI
FILA
·PRATO·
·The·
MUGELLO
POGGIO a CAIANO
CARMIGNANO
VIA BOLOGNESE
·FIESOLE·
Villa I Tatti
ARNO
·FLORENCE·
AUTOSTRADA·DEL·SOLE·
·RESTAURANTS·
·FLORENCE·Borgo Antico · Coco Lezzone ·La Carabaccia·
·Ganino's ·Sostanza·
·FIESOLE ·Le Cave di Maiano ·Il Lordo·
·S. ANDREA PERCUSSINA·
·Taverna Macchiavelli·
S. ANDREA·
in PERCUSSINA
·SAN CASCIANO·
VAL di PESA
·SIGHTS·
·CARMIGNANO ·wine·
·Villa Artimino ·FIESOLE·
·Roman ruins ·villas·
·caves ·POGGIO A CAIANO·
·Villa Medicea ·PRATO·
·Duomo ·frescoes ·THE MUGELLO ·villas of Cafaggiolo & Trebbio·

· INTRODUCTION ·

'Fiorentin mangia fagioli
Lecca piatti e tova glioli.'
The Florentine who eats beans
Licks the plates and tablecloths
(OLD TUSCAN SAYING)

Aldous Huxley called Florence a 'third rate provincial town' which is unfair. But certainly in spite of its wealth of art and culture the city sometimes seems designed to annoy the uninformed visitor. From six in the morning when the huge covered central market rings with the shouts of what sounds like the entire Florentine population, the noise of traffic and people fills the streets. VIVOLI, the best and most famous ice cream shop in Florence is busier at midnight than any other time. Museums are open only in the mornings, shop hours alter with a bewildering frequency and just when you think you have cracked the system, everything shuts at one o'clock for lunch. Grey steel shutters clang down abruptly to cover all the tempting displays of goodies, leaving formerly lively shopping streets bare and bleak. For four hours nothing moves except the occasional fly and in the summer heat of Florence (one of the hottest and most humid cities in Italy) even the flies can be a little sluggish.

The only solution is to follow the Florentine example. Rise early to shop and see the staggering variety of museums and churches and save the afternoon for a long, lazy lunch in a cool restaurant. Or picnic and siesta in the huge formal Boboli gardens behind the Pitti Palace. If you can cope with the heat explore the narrow streets lined with medieval and Renaissance palaces in the precious quiet hours between one and five o'clock. During the rest of the day whining mopeds are a constant hazard, whizzing merrily down so-called 'pedestrian only' thoroughfares and missing tourists and Florentines alike only by centimetres.

The city is not now and never has been a restful place to visit. Exhilarating, yes. Restful, no. Its centuries-long participation in a conflict between the Guelfs, who supported the Pope, and the Ghibellines, who supported the Emperor, divided the whole of Tuscany. And although by 1266 the Guelfs were the main faction in

Florence, the internal politics were still so unstable that Dante (1265~1321) compared his hometown to a sick woman, twisting and turning on her bed to ease her pain. It took Cosimo de'Medici in 1434 to initiate a period of relative stability, and it was during the rule of the Medici family, the height of the Renaissance, that Tuscan artists, sculptors and architects shaped Florence into the tightly~packed urban treasure house that it is today.

E. M. Forster called the Renaissance '...all fighting and beauty' and the fighting was not limited to politics. Pietro Torrigiano broke Michelangelo's nose in a fistfight on the steps of the Carmine church. They were arguing about the stunning frescoes by Masaccio in the Brancacci chapel. And Brunelleschi, after losing the commission to Ghiberti to sculpt the doors of Florence's Baptistry, left the city in a huff, returning only to design the famous cupola of the Duomo. His advanced ideas caused an uproar in the city but were finally realised in 1436. The raising of the massive red dome was the outstanding engineering feat of the Renaissance period. Visible for miles in all directions, its size was unmatched even by Michelangelo's dome of St. Peter's in Rome, a generation later.

To Florentine food lovers the 'bistecca fiorentina' is as much a masterpiece as Brunelleschi's dome is to architects. Sit in a crowded trattoria near Florence's huge central market and you will hear arguments as passionate about grilling the perfect steak as those about politics or art. Whether the 'fiorentina' (a steak of truly monumental proportions) should be first brushed with oil and then grilled, or never see oil at all, is an argument that can last as long as the parties involved are willing to continue. But Tuscans, and especially Florentines, will argue about anything. Preferably with the benefit of a meal and some good wine for stimulation.

The best arguments and the best food are to be found not in hyperelegant hotel restaurants with elaborately served international food but in local Florentine trattorias. Eat perhaps just a plate of the white beans of which the Florentines are notoriously so fond, simmered to a creamy smoothness in sage & garlic and then drenched in fine fruity olive oil. Or ask for a slice of roast pork off the spit, its skin crackling with rosemary and black pepper. These simple dishes served in unpretentious surroundings are the real flavour of Florence, nowhere better than in one of the little neighbourhood restaurants like LA CARABACCIA, GANINO's or SOSTANZA, sitting elbow to elbow with your fellow diners at long communal tables.

It is hard to decide the best way to enter Florence for the first time. Arriving in the main railway station of Santa Maria Novella one senses only the presence of the modern city with all its attendant modern problems = noise, traffic, smell and heat. The city of Dante & Michelangelo is as distant as the blue Appennine mountains. But drive in from the north, down the old Via Bolognese (the SS65 from Bologna) and the Florence & Tuscany of the Renaissance come to life. From the dramatic Futa Pass the road runs through the gentle Mugello valley, birthplace of Ghiotto & Fra Angelico, past some of the grandest of the Renaissance villas. First there is Michelozzi's Cafaggiolo, then Trebbio and the medieval castle of Salviati where, in the 17th century, Jacopo Salviati received the severed head of his mistress as a New Year's gift from his wife. The road then leads past Sir Harold Acton's Villa La Pietra, with one of the most beautiful formal Italian gardens in Tuscany. And along the Via Bolognese for the last stretch Roman Fiesole rises on its villa & cypress covered hill to the east. Finally Brunelleschi's famous red dome comes into view, dwarfing every building for miles around, and you are in Florence.

SOUPS

S is for soup, or in Tuscany Z is for zuppa ~ any soup served over bread, as most are. They can vary widely from the simplest clear broth with fresh herbs used to boil a chicken, to zuppa di agnello in which there is only enough 'zuppa' left to soak the bread under a rich stew of lamb and tomatoes. The key to ordering or cooking a good Tuscan soup is the season ~ check the market for best buys and choose your recipe accordingly. In Tuscany it is stale bread that thickens soups, not flour or pasta and usually a jug of olive oil is served as dressing.

PORRI

PEPOLINO-O-TIMO
£ 800 AL
MAZZO

OGGI
FAGIOLI
CECI COTTI

PEPE RONI
PICCANTE

ROSMARINO

SALVIA

· LA · CARABACCIA ·

E ach day at La Carabaccia in Florence, Luciano Ghimassi serves different, carefully researched Florentine dishes, largely based on ingredients produced by himself and his family. His intimate little restaurant is always packed with locals and booking is essen~ tial unless you are the friend of a regular customer.

· LA CARABACCIA ·
—— Onion soup (4)——

This dish is just one of many Tuscan dishes that form part of a centuries~old debate. In 1533 Catherine de'Medici went to France to marry the future Henry II, taking with her a retinue of chefs and so starting the debate about the origin of certain dishes. Some are internationally iden~ tified with French cuisine but the Tuscans claim them for their own. Who now knows whether Catherine and her chefs changed the course of French cooking with dishes such as anitra all'arancia (canard à l'orange) or whether the inspir~ ation came from the French and filtered back to Italy with lonely Tuscan chefs returning home? Perhaps Catherine's chefs, homesick for their Tuscan cypresses, cooked dishes like carabaccia, which later evolved into the ubiquitous soup à l'oignon of every French bistro. This first recipe is certainly of Renaissance origin, with the characteristic thickening of crushed almonds.

· RENAISSANCE VERSION ·

2 LB 2 OZ / 1 KG ONIONS, FINELY SLICED
4 OZ /100 G ALMONDS, SKINNED &
    POUNDED TO A PASTE IN A MORTAR
1 TBSP CASTER SUGAR
4 TBSP OLIVE OIL
WHITE WINE VINEGAR
CINNAMON STICK
1 3/4 PT/1 LTR STOCK
PINCH WHITE PEPPER
PINCH SALT
POWDERED CINNAMON (OPTIONAL)
4 SLICES BREAD

Put the crushed almonds and the cinnamon stick in enough vinegar to cover, leave about 1 hour, heat the oil in a medium~sized pan, saute the onions in it until soft, using more oil if necessary. Rinse the almond paste in a sieve and add to the onions a tablespoon at a time until they are well blended. When the mixture is smooth add the sugar, pow~ dered cinnamon if liked, white pepper, salt and stock. Cook for a further 30 minutes. Put a slice of bread that has been grilled crisp and brown into each bowl, pour the soup over.

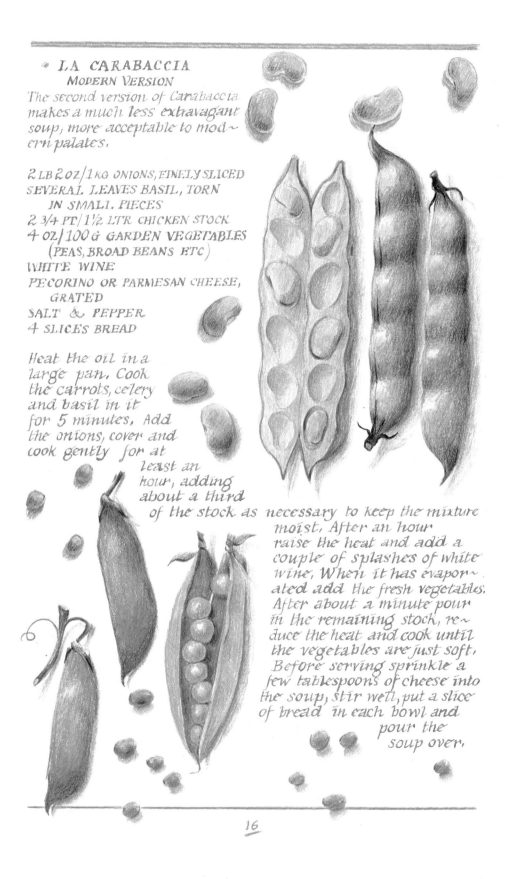

• LA CARABACCIA
MODERN VERSION

The second version of Carabaccia makes a much less extravagant soup, more acceptable to modern palates.

2 LB 2 OZ / 1 KG ONIONS, FINELY SLICED
SEVERAL LEAVES BASIL, TORN
   IN SMALL PIECES
2 3/4 PT / 1 1/2 LTR CHICKEN STOCK
4 OZ / 100 G GARDEN VEGETABLES
   (PEAS, BROAD BEANS ETC)
WHITE WINE
PECORINO OR PARMESAN CHEESE,
   GRATED
SALT & PEPPER
4 SLICES BREAD

Heat the oil in a large pan. Cook the carrots, celery and basil in it for 5 minutes. Add the onions, cover and cook gently for at least an hour, adding about a third of the stock as necessary to keep the mixture moist. After an hour raise the heat and add a couple of splashes of white wine. When it has evaporated add the fresh vegetables. After about a minute pour in the remaining stock, reduce the heat and cook until the vegetables are just soft. Before serving sprinkle a few tablespoons of cheese into the soup, stir well, put a slice of bread in each bowl and pour the soup over.

food never reflected the con~ flict, unless perhaps it had an extra zest.

· TRIPPA alla FIORENTINA ·

— Florentine Tripe (4) —

You, too, may be wary of tripe, but the Florentines have an undeniable way with it. Try it, you might be converted.

1 ¾ LB /800 G TRIPE, READY COOKED

1 LB 2 OZ /500 G TOMATOES, PEELED & ROUGHLY CHOPPED

1 ½ TSP MARJORAM

1 ¼ OZ /30 G PANCETTA (OR FATTY HAM)

3 ~4 TBSP OLIVE OIL

2 CELERY STICKS

1 CARROT

SALT & PEPPER

1 ONION

The Trattoria Sostanza op~ ened in 1869 and is still one of the best~known working~men's cafes in Florence. Go there to eat the huge bistec~ ca fiorentina & sit at long com~ munal tables where it is un~ possible not to share your conversation with half the restaurant. According to one customer who had been eat~ ing there regularly for 40 years, the two owners who had the cafe previously once had a terrible row & for years never spoke to each other. One worked in the front of the restaurant, the other at the back. Communication was only through waiters like Mario, who has himself been there for 50 years. But the

Put the tripe in a big saucepan with half the onion and a celery stick. Cover with water and boil for 10~15 minutes. Meanwhile finely chop the re~ maining onion and celery & the carrot and pancetta and cook gently in the oil in a flame~proof casserole. Drain and slice the tripe into small, fine strips about 2 in/2.5 cm long. When the onion is slightly coloured, add the tomatoes, tripe and seasoning. Cover & continue to cook over a low heat. After 30 minutes remove the lid, turn up the heat and cook until the sauce thickens (about 10 minutes), stirring occasionally to ensure that the tripe does not stick & burn. Serve with plenty of grated parmesan.

· TORTINO di CARCIOFI ·
Artichoke omelette

'Carciofi' is Italian for arti~
chokes, and if there is one
way to eat them that is bet~
ter than just boiling them
and dipping them in good
oil, this is it. The artichokes
should be young, preferably
Italian, the leaves closely
packed at the end of long
thin stems.

___

2 EGGS PER PERSON
2~3 ARTICHOKES PER PERSON,
   DEPENDING ON SIZE
¼ PT/150 ML GOOD OLIVE OIL
CLOVE GARLIC
2~3 TBSP. FRESH PARSLEY,
   FINELY CHOPPED
SALT & PEPPER
  JUICE OF 1 LEMON

Peel off any tough outer
leaves on the artichokes and,
if using non~Italian ones,
trim away the chokes. Slice
the 'flowers' thinly from the
top down through the stem,
and soak for 15 minutes in
water and lemon juice. Heat
the oil in a frying pan with
the garlic. Drain the arti~
choke slices and pat dry.
Put them in the pan with
the oil, cover and leave
the artichokes to simmer
over a low heat, turning once
or twice. When they are gol~
den brown add the eggs,
beaten with the salt, pepper
and parsley. Continue cooking
over a medium heat until
the eggs are set, stirring
all the time to prevent
burning. At the Trattoria
Sostanza they serve their
tortinos with a squeeze
of fresh lemon juice and
plenty of crusty bread to
mop up the delicious juice.

___

When using non~Italian
artichokes be sure they are
very young and small and
use only the most tender
inner leaves.

· GANINO'S ·

Ganino's is the place where poets rub shoulders with film stars, and are served by the entire Bernadoni family (most of whom could pass for film stars themselves). In spring the tagliatelle with wild asparagus is worth dieting for, and all year round the crostini di fegatini are the best in Tuscany.

CROSTINI di FEGATINI
Chicken livers on toast (6)

Crostini probably appear on every antipasto menu in every Tuscan trattoria, but all too often they arrive as gritty grey paste on soggy bread. At Ganino's the bread is first grilled over an open wood fire, then brushed with good green olive oil and at the last minute annointed with this hot creamy mixture of chicken livers, sharpened with capers and anchovy.

6 CHICKEN LIVERS, CLEANED
1 ANCHOVY, FINELY CHOPPED
1 TSP TOMATO PUREE
WINEGLASS WHITE WINE
BUTTER
2 TBSP CAPERS, CRUSHED IN A
  MORTAR
10 OR MORE SLICES FRENCH
  BAGUETTE BREAD
1 MEDIUM ONION, FINELY
  CHOPPED
CHICKEN STOCK
GRATED PARMESAN

Melt some butter in a small saucepan and saute the onion in it until transparent. Add the chicken livers and break them up with a fork as they begin to colour. After a few minutes pour in the wine and allow to evaporate slowly. When evaporated add the anchovy and capers, and the tomato puree mixed in a little hot stock. Continue to cook for about 15 minutes, adding more stock when necessary to keep the mixture very creamy. Just before serving beat the livers well (or whisk in a food processor) and serve very hot on toasted bread with a generous sprinkling of freshly grated parmesan or pecorino cheese over the top.

· C O C O · L E Z Z O N E ·

In their minute kitchen off an equally tiny white~tiled restaurant, the Paoli family manage to produce some of the best traditional Tuscan cooking in Florence.

· FARFALLINE con PISELLI ·
Pasta butterflies
with fresh peas (4)

Theoretically, this is not a difficult dish to make. Stand next to a field of fresh peas with a frying pan in your hand in which is simmering gently a generous handful of pale pink prosciutto and perhaps a few finely chopped green spring onions. Wait until the peas are barely ripe ~ still tiny and bright green in their pods. At that precise moment start shelling them straight into the pan, toss them quickly in the sauce, pour onto a bowl of freshly cooked farfalline (butterfly~shaped pasta) and run with them to the nearest table. If you do this and they were good peas to start with, they might, perhaps, taste as good as the peas and pasta served at Coco Lezzone. Failing a field of peas, take:

CocoLezzone

· Farfalline con Piselli
May '84

20 PASTA 'BUTTERFLIES' PER
   PERSON
2 LB/900 G FRESHLY SHELLED
   PEAS ~ TRY ONE RAW, IF IT IS
   NOT SWEET, ADD A GENEROUS
   PINCH OF SUGAR WHEN COOKING
4 OZ/100 G PROSCIUTTO OR GOOD
   COOKED HAM SLICED IN THIN STRIPS
2 SPRING ONIONS, FINELY CHOPPED
1 TBSP OLIVE OIL
SALT & PEPPER

Put the pasta to cook in a large pan of boiling salted water. Heat the oil in a frying pan. Saute the onions gently in the oil until soft but not brown. Add the peas (and sugar if neces~ sary) and a tablespoon or two of water. Cook them as quickly as possible, about 10 ~15 min~ utes (less if they are small & very tender). About 5 minutes before they are ready add the ham and allow to heat through. Pour over the pasta which should be cooked and drained ready for serving. Serve immediately

• FAGIOLI al FIASCO •
Beans in a Chianti bottle (6)

This must be one of the oldest and simplest of Tuscan dishes. It is excellent

barbecue food but first drink your Chianti...

12 OZ/350 G FRESH WHITE TUSCAN,
   HARICOT OR CANNELLINI BEANS
4 TBSP GOOD OLIVE OIL
5 ~6 SAGE LEAVES
2 CLOVES GARLIC, CRUSHED

Having drunk the Chianti, cut the straw wrapping off the bottle (capacity should be about 3 pints/1½ ltr) but keep it to use as a stopper. Rinse out the bottle and fill it about ½ to ⅔ full with beans (the beans need room to swell). Add the oil, sage leaves, garlic and about 1½ cups of water. Stuff the straw loosely in the top of the flask so that the water can ev~ aporate ~ to achieve their char~ acteristic creamy taste, the beans must absorb oil, not water. Put the bottle beside or above the embers of the fire for 3 ~5 hours. Failing a campfire put the bottle in a warm place, such as an airing cupboard, the warm place on a stove, or beside the boiler or a solid fuel cooker. Leave until the water has evaporated and the beans have absorbed the oil. Serve hot or cold with plenty of salt & freshly ground black pepper and a jug of good fruity olive oil to pour over.

21

·LETIZIA·

Letizia Volpi is an artist living and working in Florence, and a passionate collector of old recipes for Tuscan sweets. Perhaps one day she will write her own book on the subject. In the meantime she is content to delight all her friends and family by cooking six times the usual quantity for recipes such as this one. And there is an added bonus. One evening of cooking crunchy CENCI is enough to fill the house for days with the delicious smell of vanilla and icing sugar.

· CENCI ·
— Fried pastry twists —

'Cenci' means 'stuff' or scraps of fabric used for dusting and cleaning. Like its fabric counter~

part, the pastry comes in all shapes and sizes, from huge pasty handkerchiefs and long strips tied in bows and lover's knots, to the heart~shaped dolce d'amore made by Letizia Volpi. They are generally popular at carnival time, just after Christmas.

9 oz/250 G PLAIN WHITE FLOUR
1 oz/25 G BUTTER, JUST MELTED
1 oz/25 G GRANULATED SUGAR
1 EGG
3 TBSP VIN SANTO ~ VIN SANTO IS
  AN ITALIAN SHERRY~LIKE WINE
  BUT YOU CAN USE SHERRY OR RUM
1 TSP VANILLA POWDER
PINCH SALT
OIL FOR DEEP FRYING

Make a little volcano of sifted flour with a crater in the middle. Into this put the egg, salt, sugar, vanilla and butter. Gently work this into a dough with your hands. When the dough begins to get stiff, moisten with a little vin santo, as the dough should always be quite pliable. Knead well, cover with a cloth and leave in a cool place to rest. After about an hour, roll the dough out very thinly and cut into whatever shapes you like. Probably the most trad~ itional is a strip about 8 in/ 20.5 cm long and ½ in/3 cm wide tied in a bow or knot.

Deep fry these pieces, 2 or 3 at a time, in hot oil until they puff up & turn golden brown. Drain on paper towels and sift icing sugar over the tops. They can be eaten hot or cold and keep well in an airtight container.

The famous grey stone 'PIETRA SERENA' from which half the buildings in Flo~ rence are constructed, comes from the quarries near Fiesole, le Cave di Maiano. The trat~ toria of the same name is no longer the haven for workers from the nearby quarries that it once was. A more international crowd comes now for the stunning views of cypresses and villas in the Fiesolan hills, rather than for their essential even~ ing meal. But there are still some very good traditional dishes to be found on the menu if you know your trad~ itions and are willing (and able) to ask about them.

· PAPPA al POMODORO ·
Tomato and bread soup (8)

This thick, richly to~ mato~tasting soup that was once almost the porridge of Tus~ cany is one such tra~ ditional dish. If you make sure the tomatoes and basil are fresh, the bread stale and the garlic lavish, you cannot go far wrong. It can be, and is, served hot or cold, tepid or, less authentically, with ice cubes and topped with a generous handful of fresh chopped basil. (Failing basil, other fresh herbs can be almost as good ~ try thyme, rosemary or parsley.)

8 FL OZ/225 ML VERY GOOD OLIVE OIL
3~4 CLOVES GARLIC, CRUSHED
8 LEAVES BASIL, OR MORE IF YOU LIKE
1 LB 2 OZ/500 G TOMATOES,
    PEELED & CHOPPED
1 LB 2 OZ/500 G WHOLE WHEAT BREAD
    1 MEDIUM LEEK,
      FINELY CHOPPED
    2¼ PT/1.4 LTR STOCK
    SALT & PEPPER
    (½ TSP CRUSHED
    CHILI PEPPER ~
    OPTIONAL)

Heat the oil in a deep pan & sauté the leek, gar~ lic (& chili if using). When they are soft, add the tomatoes & basil & boil for 5~10 minutes. Then add the stock, salt & pepper. When the soup is boiling add the stale bread torn into small pieces. Cook for 2 minutes, cover & let stand for an hour. Then mix well, pour on some fresh oil and serve with parmesan.

25

· MASHA · INNOCENTI ·

Masha Innocenti runs a cook~ery school in Florence for foreigners pin~ing to learn the secrets of Italian cooking. She comes from a whole family of Tuscan cooks and her culinary inspiration is as much from a Lucch~esan mother as from a cordon bleu chef's course.

CONIGLIO con OLIVE NERE
—Tuscan rabbit— with black olives (6)

This recipe for rabbit with black olives is especially typical of the region around Lucca where both rabbits & excellent olives are plentiful.

3 LB/1.4 KG RABBIT WASHED & CUT INTO PIECES
2 CLOVES GARLIC
8 FL OZ/225 ML OLIVE OIL
2 OZ/60 G BUTTER
4 FL OZ/110 ML WHITE WINE
1 TBSP TOMATO PASTE
6 TBSP BLACK OLIVES
8 FL OZ/225 ML STOCK
SALT & BLACK PEPPER

Remove skin from the garlic cloves and slash each clove halfway through. Heat the oil and butter or margarine in a large sauce~pan or fire~proof casserole. Add the garlic and rabbit & brown on all sides over a medium heat. When brown add the wine, turn up the heat & let it evaporate. Then lower the heat, add the tomato paste and stock, cover and cook over a medium heat for 15 minutes. Season to taste, add the black olives & cook for another 25 ~ 30 minutes until the meat is tender & has turned a light pink. Add more stock if the stew appears to be in dan~ger of drying out.

• POLLO in FRICASSEA •
Chicken in lemon sauce (6)

This classic method of cooking chicken in
lemon sauce is equally good with loin
of veal cut into pieces.

3 LB / 1.4 KG CHICKEN, CLEANED,
DRIED AND CUT IN PIECES

2 OZ / 60 G BUTTER

4 FL OZ / 110 ML OLIVE OIL

SMALL WHITE ONION, CHOPPED

JUICE OF 1 LEMON

2 TBSP FLOUR

3 EGG YOLKS

SALT & WHITE PEPPER

2 TBSP CHOPPED PARSLEY

6 FL OZ / 165 ML ~ 8 FL OZ / 220 ML STOCK

Heat the oil and butter in a shallow heat-proof
casserole, add the onion and saute gently until
transparent. Add the chicken pieces and brown
well all over. Pour in about 4 fl oz / 110 ml of
stock, cover and cook gently for 15~20 minutes,
adding more stock if necessary to prevent drying
out or burning. Mix the flour to a paste in 2 fl oz /
50 ml of stock & stir slowly into the liquid in
the casserole to thicken it. Season to taste. Beat the yolks
& lemon juice together. When the chicken is cooked,
in approximately 40 minutes, remove casserole from
the heat & add the yolks & lemon juice mixture,
blending in well. Add parsley & serve.

" TORTA della NONNA "
Grandmother's cake (8)

Grandmothers all over Tuscany make this cake, and so do many restaurants, cafés and pastry~ shops. Basically it is a del~ iciously rich and creamy flan filled with confectioner's cus~ tard and covered with a mixture of pastry, toasted al~ monds, pine nuts and icing sugar, but there are dozens of variations on the same theme.

FOR THE CREAM:
2 EGG YOLKS
1¼ OZ / 35 G PLAIN
   WHITE FLOUR
1 PT / 575 ML MILK
2¼ OZ / 75 G CASTER
   SUGAR
SLIVERED ALMONDS
  & PINE NUTS
   FOR TOPPING

FOR PASTRY:
12 ½ OZ / 350 G
  PLAIN WHITE FLOUR
1 EGG & 1 EGG YOLK
2¾ OZ / 75 G CASTER
   SUGAR
4 OZ / 100 G BUTTER
1 ½ TSP BAKING POWDER

First make the cream. Heat the milk until it starts to boil, remove from the heat. Beat the yolks and sugar together until they form a ribbon. Stir in the flour, blending well. Add one tbsp of the hot milk to the yolk~sugar mixture and blend in well with a wooden spoon. Add the mixture to the milk and return to the heat, stirring until the cream thickens. When thickened, pour into a clean bowl and brush the surface with some melted butter to stop a skin forming. Allow to cool.

In the meantime toast a gen~ erous handful of almonds and pine nuts on a baking sheet until they are sligtly browned.

To make the pastry sift the flour and baking powder into a mound on a pastry-board or work surface, make a well in the middle and put all the other ingredients into it. Work every~ thing into a dough with your hands. Form into a ball and chill in the refrigerator for 30 minutes. When ready to use, cut the dough in half, roll out one half into a circle ⅛ in/ 3 mm thick and place on an 8 in/20.5 cm greased pie plate, making sure that there is about ½ in/1 cm hanging over the plate's edge. Pour the cream onto the pastry base, making sure that the middle is some~ what higher than the edges. Fold the pastry rim inwards and brush with some water. Roll the remaining piece of dough out to fit and place gently on top of the cream. Press well onto the pastry border & trim off any excess. Top with the almonds and pine nuts and bake in a preheated oven at 350°F/180°C / Gas 4 for 25 ~30 minutes until golden brown. Cool and sift with plenty of icing sugar before serving.

> * They serve a very good ver~ sion of this sweet at the little, crowded trattoria 'Il Lordo' off the main square in Fiesole.

At the Borgo Antico in Florence they serve a delicious salad of freshly shelled 'bacelli' (broad beans) and equal parts pec~ orino cheese & slivers of prosciutto. Everything is then tossed in lots of good olive oil and served with fresh ground pepper.

At Il Cibreo in Flo~ rence, a trattoria near the Santa Am~ brogio market behind Santa Croce, they mix fresh ricotta cheese with marjoram, grate pecorino cheese on top & grill until golden brown.

~4~
Simple Dishes
Some of the best food in Tuscany is also the ea~ siest to prepare.

The traditional ending to a Tuscan country meal is a bowl of pears, peeled & served with pec~ orino cheese. Eaten young pecorino can be rubbery, but ask for piccante & you will get a cheese a bit like parmes~ an that goes well with ripe pears.

Fettunta is toast (usually grilled ov~ er an open fire) that is rubbed with garlic & drenched in olive oil & sea salt. It is called Brus~ chetta when topped with a mix~ ture of raw tomatoes & fresh basil.

29

Niccolo Macchiavelli is one of the least liked and most misunderstood personalities in Tuscan history, probably because he made the mistake of telling the truth in his book, The Prince. His name is synonymous with treachery & deviousness. The Albergaccio Macchiavelli just outside Florence is doing much to rectify that. Directly opposite the villa (open to the public) where the original Machiavelli spent his 15-year exile from Florence, this little trattoria serves good wine, good garlic bread and good Fagioli all'uccelletto.

· FAGIOLI all'UCCELLETTO ·
Beans cooked like small birds (4)

This famous Tuscan dish is perhaps called 'all'uccelletto' because an uccelletto is a small bird and these beans are cooked in the same way that small birds are cooked during the hunting season. The recipe comes from another Macchiavelli, Leonardo claims to be one of the last surviving members of the family and is himself a political thinker, although more usually the maker of vin santo and fine CARMIGNANO wines. The excellent Carmignano wines are made in a small area near the Medici villa of Poggio a Caiano north of Florence. They are not widely available outside Italy, but there is a wide selection at the little enoteca (wine store) in the centre of Poggio a Caiano, among them Leonardo's gold-medal winning Vino Carmignano from the Fattoria Ambra that he manages.

2 LB 2OZ / 1 KG FRESH WHITE TOSCANELLI BEANS OR

14 OZ / 400 G DRIED WHITE BEANS

14 OZ / 400 G PEELED TOMATOES

2~3 CLOVES GARLIC

OLIVE OIL

5 OR MORE FRESH SAGE LEAVES

SALT & FRESHLY GROUND BLACK PEPPER

Soak the dried beans overnight & then rinse, or if using fresh beans shell & wash. Boil in slightly salted water for 30~40 minutes. Heat several tablespoons of olive oil in a medium-sized heat-proof casserole. Brown the garlic, sage & pepper in the oil and then add the beans, stirring for a few minutes to allow the flavours to blend. Add the tomatoes, chopped roughly, salt to taste & continue cooking covered for about 15 minutes.

NB. These beans can be turned into a Tuscan version of wieners or bangers & beans if you sauté 2 spicy sausages per person over a low heat until browned, remove from pan and continue recipe as above, using the sausage fat instead of olive oil. About 15 minutes before the end of cooking, return the sausages to the pan and add four tablespoons of red wine.

ABOVE: Grapes for VIN SANTO drying on straw mats in the attic of Leonardo's farmhouse near Poggio a Caiano.

and is traditionally served as a dessert wine with Biscotti di Prato (page 36).

- ANITRA con VIN SANTO - Duck with vin santo (4)

Each Tuscan winemaker makes his own version of vin santo or 'holy wine', but because of the painstaking and lengthy pro~ duction it is extremely difficult to buy outside Tuscany. Made from semi·dried grapes, it must be aged for a minimum of 3 years before emerging in~ to the sunlight as vin santo. At its best it has a wonderfully smoky aromatic flavour rather like fine old sherry or Madeira

1 4 lb / 1.8 KG DUCK WITH GIBLETS
2 WINE GLASSES VIN SANTO (OR
    GOOD MEDIUM DRY SHERRY)
1 ONION
1 STICK CELERY
5 OZ / 150 G CHOPPED PROSCIUTTO
    OR FATTY HAM
1 CARROT
4 SAGE LEAVES
OLIVE OIL
SALT
WHITE PEPPER
14 OZ / 400 ML CHICKEN OR BEEF STOCK

Chop the onion, celery, carrot, sage and prosciutto and put in a heat~ proof casserole with the oil

32

over a medium heat.
When transparent and
soft add the duck, cut in
pieces, and brown on all
sides, Season with salt and white
pepper and pour in the vin santo.
Cover and cook for several minutes over a low heat. Then add ½
the stock and the finely chopped
duck liver. Cover again and continue to cook for about an hour,
adding a few tablespoons of stock
from time to time. The resulting
sauce should not be too liquid.
It is best to let the dish cool and
then skim off the fat, as duck
tends to give off a lot of fat.
Reheat after skimming and serve
the sauce over plain flat maccheroni, the pieces of duck to follow
as a separate course perhaps
with fagioli all'uccelletto or,
for a less heavy meal, this dish
of spinach and swiss chard.

One of the most outstanding
vin santos in Tuscany is from
the AVIGNONESI estate. They
sell only 1000 bottles a year
but also serve it in their splendid restaurant 'LA CASANUOVA'
near Chianciano.

BIETOLE & SPINACI
• CON PINOLI •
—Spinach & swiss chard—
with pine nuts (4)

1 LB 4 OZ / ½ KG SPINACH, TRIMMED
  OR EQUIVALENT BEETTOPS
1 LB 4 OZ / ½ KG SWISS CHARD,
  TRIMMED
1 GARLIC CLOVE
SMALL HANDFUL PINE NUTS
SMALL HANDFUL RAISINS
SALT & PEPPER
OLIVE OIL

Boil the spinach and swiss chard
in separate pans of salted water
until just tender (about 15 minutes). Drain both vegetables well
and squeeze into a ball. Chop
them coarsely and put them in
a frying pan in which the oil,
garlic, pine nuts and raisins have
been gently simmering. Sauté
for several minutes to blend the
flavours, and serve hot with
freshly ground black pepper.

33

34

At the end of the last century when the art historian Bernard Berenson was a young man, he rode out on his bicycle every morning from his Florence pensione, his pockets filled with candles to light the obscure corners of unknown churches all over Tuscany, returning in the dusk to write up discoveries that would one day make him famous. In later, more prosperous years, his charming villa, I TATTI, just outside Florence, became the focal point for all the visiting members of the literary and artistic set. Now it is a Renaissance study centre (visits for ordinary tourists can be arranged through the Italian Tourist Board in Florence) and lucky Harvard University students can freely prowl the formal gardens. And equally freely supply a Renaissance recipe like this one. It is good served with a selection of other Tuscan antipasti such as crostini, prosciutto and olives, or a salad of beans & cheese.

· INVOLTINI di SALVIA ·
Sage Leaf Rolls

It is difficult to gauge quantities for these little hors d'oeuvres as it depends on the greed of the people eating them. Essentially the recipe is this: for each sage roll take two large sage leaves & one anchovy (the anchovy should be soaked in milk for 30 minutes to remove salt). Make these into a 'sandwich' with the anchovy in the middle, roll them up & secure with a toothpick. Each of these is then dipped first in beaten egg, then in flour, & finally deep fried in hot oil until crisp & puffed up.

35

· BISCOTTI di PRATO ·
Prato biscuits (1 lb)

Probably the most com-
mon conclusion to a
dinner in Tuscany is the
arrival of a plate of these
curiously hard, oval biscuits.
Dunked liberally in a glass of
vin santo, they are magically
transformed into a surprisingly
moreish dessert. They should be
hard and dry to start with
(and will keep for months in
a tightly closed container)
and in fact the bakers in Prato
put ammonium bicarbonate, an
old-fashioned leavening agent,
into their biscuits to ensure an
extra long hard life. In Italy
Prato biscuits are seldom served
without vin santo to accompany
them. However if vin santo is
unavailable you can use a good
sweet sherry instead.

✳ Biscotti di Prato are also
available commercially in
packages, but lack the flavour
& consistency of these home-made
biscuits.

1 LB 2 OZ/500 G CASTER SUGAR
1 LB 2 OZ/500 G WHITE FLOUR
7 OZ/200 G PEELED ALMONDS
5 OZ/150 G PINENUTS
4 EGGS, BEATEN

1 TSP GRATED
ORANGE PEEL
½ TSP VANILLA
EXTRACT
½ TSP BAKING
POWDER
SALT
BUTTER

Preheat oven to 375°F/190°C/
Gas 5. Toast the almonds in
the oven for a couple of minutes and chop roughly with
the pinenuts. Sift the flour
onto a pastry board or work surface. Make a well in the middle
and pour in eggs, baking powder, sugar and a pinch of salt.
Work to a smooth consistency
with your hands and then mix
in nuts. Roll pieces of the dough
into long 'fingers'. Place on a
greased, floured baking sheet
& bake in the oven for about 15
minutes. Remove & slice dough
fingers on the diagonal, about
½ in/1 cm thick, and
bake for another
25 minutes
until
brown.

· BORGO · ANTICO ·

The little birreria, Borgo Antico, in Florence's Piazza Santa Spirito serves a modern version of an authentic Renaissance Tuscan dish & definitely without the original's near disastrous consequences.

CIBREO

Cibreo was one of Catherine de'Medici's favourite dishes. There is a story that one day after eating too many heaped platefuls she nearly died of indigestion. Considering that Cibreo was once made with the livers, kidneys, testicles & crests of cockerels, this seems hardly surprising!

1 LB 2 OZ / 500 G CHICKEN LIVER, ROUGHLY CHOPPED
1 SMALL ONION OR LEEK VERY FINELY CHOPPED
2 OZ / 50 G BUTTER
2 EGG YOLKS
JUICE OF ½ LEMON
FLOUR
SALT & PEPPER
A LITTLE CHICKEN STOCK

Melt the butter in a medium-sized pan, saute the onion in it until soft but not brown. Roll the liver in flour, add to the pan with salt & pepper and cook over a low heat, adding a few tablespoons of stock as necessary to keep the mixture moist and creamy. Meanwhile lightly beat the yolks & lemon juice together. When the liver is just cooked through, take from the heat and stir in the egg mixture. Leave for two minutes and serve with toast as a light first course or luncheon dish.

· PAN di RAMERINO ·
— Rosemary buns —

The fragrant and sticky 'pan di Ramerino' is a famous sweet bun popular with Florentine children during the Easter holidays. To make these buns add 3 oz/75g of sugar to the bread ingredients on page 67. Work into a dough and leave to rise in a warm place until doubled in size. Then put the dough on a table and mix into it 1½ wine glasses of olive oil in which 2 sprigs of fresh rosemary have been slowly heated for 10~15 minutes. Add 4 oz/100g of raisins and 2 tbsp of finely chopped rosemary leaves to the dough and form into buns of 3in/7.5cm in diameter. Make a cross on the top with a pair of scissors, brush with beaten egg and bake until golden (20~30mins) in an oven preheated to 400°F/200°C/Gas 6.

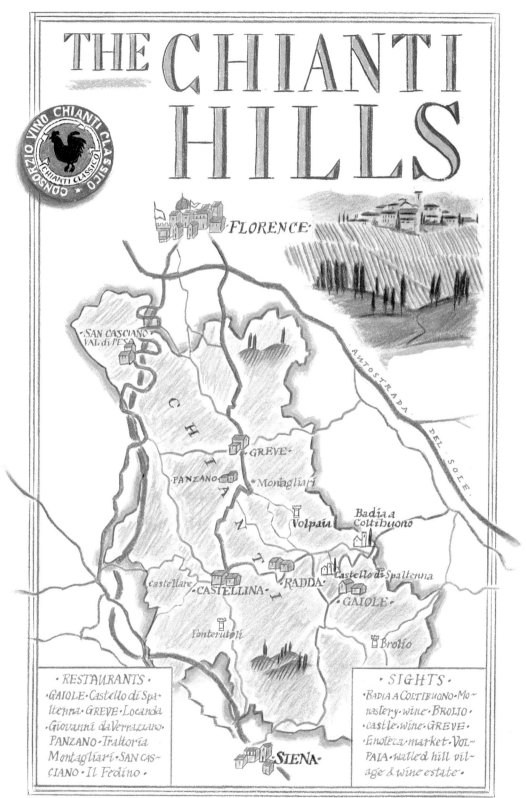

THE CHIANTI HILLS

CONSORZIO VINO CHIANTI CLASSICO · CHIANTI CLASSICO

FLORENCE

AUTOSTRADA DEL SOLE

SAN CASCIANO VAL di PESA

C H I A N T I

GREVE

PANZANO · Montagliari

Volpaia

Badia a Coltibuono

Castello di Spaltenna

castellare · CASTELLINA · RADDA · GAIOLE

Fonterutoli

Brolio

SIENA

· RESTAURANTS ·
· GAIOLE · Castello di Spaltenna · GREVE · Locanda Giovanni da Verrazzano · PANZANO · Trattoria Montagliari · SAN CASCIANO · Il Fedino ·

· SIGHTS ·
· BADIA A COLTIBUONO · Monastery · wine · BROLIO · castle · wine · GREVE · Enoteca · market · VOLPAIA · walled hill village & wine estate ·

· INTRODUCTION ·

The Chianti wine district of Tuscany stretches from north of Florence, west to Pisa, south as far as Chiusi and east to Arezzo. But the soul of Chianti is the area of pine-clad hills rambling for 30~40 miles between Florence and Siena. This is the domain of the Chianti 'League' founded by feudal barons in the thirteenth century to protect their interests, one of the earliest regions to put controls on wine and an area almost constantly at war during the middle ages.

There is little evidence now of Chianti's turbulent past. The splendid views of vineyards and castles made famous in Renaissance paintings are more likely to be disturbed by the buzz of mopeds and Fiats than battles. Even the Castello di Volpaia, a medieval hill castle that was the scene of many violent clashes between Florence and Siena is now better known for its excellent Chianti and for the art exhibitions put on in the twelfth century church.

The Castello di Volpaia is one of the prettiest of the walled hill villages, with a reputation for good wine dating back to the fifteenth century, but throughout the region there are castles and villages unchanged since medieval times, most selling their own wines, delicate olive oils and local products like the soaps and colognes made from olive oil and local lavender (called 'spigo' in the Chianti region), at the hill town of Fonterutoli. Tiny dusty roads link vineyards to yellow-ochre farmhouses; farms to walled villages and villages eventually to bigger wine towns. Originally the only red 'Chianti' towns were Radda, Castellina and Gaiole. Now the main market town of Greve, on the stunning Via Chiantigiana (the SS222), is also included. A lively wine festival is held every September in Greve's charming seventeenth-century Piazza Matteoti and the town's Enoteca di Gallo Nero sells a complete selection of Chianti Classico, the DOC-registered wine identified by a black cockerel on the label. The Gallo Nero 'Classico' wines are not the only good Chiantis however. The black cockerel guarantees only that the wine has met the standards set by the DOC, Denominazione di Origine Controllata, originally set up by a group of Chianti producers, the Italian equivalent of the French Appellation Contrôle system.

The history of Chianti wine is almost as long as that of the district itself. By the time the straw-covered flask became famous (around 1860) it had been made for at least six centuries. It is possible that monks were the first Chianti producers. Certainly the monks at the beautiful abbey of Badia a Coltibuono (now a wine estate) were making wine at least as early as the twelfth century and continued to do so for hundreds of years. At the Castellare estate of Castellina grapes were grown for wine long before Lorenzo de' Medici ruled Florence in the fifteenth century. Monks from the nearby San Niccolò monastery worked the hard, stoney terrain with hoes in vineyards that are still producing good wine.

Chianti has evolved and changed considerably over the centuries. In the nineteenth century Baron Ricasoli of the Castello di Brolio established a basic 'recipe' for the blend of white and red grapes that would give modern Chianti its characteristic taste. Today it is one of the most famous wines in the world but not without certain problems. Disagreements on quality control amongst its producers and in some cases a lack of interest in modern techniques and an overuse of easy-to-grow white grapes have made a few Chiantis pale and insipid. This has damaged the wine's overall reputation. Fortunately Chianti is still popular thanks to the constant efforts of young wine-makers to improve and refine the taste of their wine while still maintaining its original rich quality.

There is the same diversity in the food and cooking of the Chianti region. A good meal can be as simple as a slice of creamy fresh ricotta and a handful of tiny jewel-

·FOUR·CHIANTI·TOWNS·

GAIOLE

RADDA

CASTELLINA

GREVE

42

red wild strawberries picked and eaten still warm on a steep hillside. A village trattoria may serve its own salty pecorino cheese and rough young Chianti with a dish of fresh olives from local trees, or a plate of home-made pasta with just a chunk of crusty bread to mop up the plain sauce of oil and sage leaves. Or elaborate Renaissance dishes fit for a Medici banquet may be elegantly served with a mellow, aged Chianti 'riserva' in a castle's cool vaulted dining hall. This is the country where a whole roast wild boar is not an uncommon feast during the autumn hunting season. In fact the name 'Chianti' is popularly believed to stem from the Latin 'clangor', a word for the loud blast a trumpet makes on a baronial hunting party.

More than any other part of Tuscany, wine in the Chianti region is an inescapable part of life. The people there eat, drink, talk and sleep it. They serve food to complement wine rather than the reverse. Despite this enthusiasm and such a good end product, there is little formal wine tourism in the district. However most wine estates welcome visitors and more frequently now have a trattoria or even more rustic osteria on the premises where both local wine and good simple food are served beside views of vineyards, cypresses and medieval castles.

Next to an eleventh~century village church on one of the vine~covered hills above Gaiole in Chianti is the Castello di Spaltenna, a beautiful and serene hotel cum restaurant. If you are lucky and go on the right day, Anna, the local cook might be there. She comes up regularly from Gaiole and in season cooks local dishes at the Castello that are seldom found outside Tuscany. She also has the Italian knack of making gnocchi & fresh pasta seem easy ~ make a pile of flour, put 5 eggs in the middle, work it a bit with enough water and there's your pasta . . .

· PANZANELLA ·
Bread & tomato salad (6)

This is the kind of recipe, if you can call it a recipe, that sounds awful and tastes delicious. Like many of Tuscany's deceptively simple dishes, it relies on perfectly fresh ingredients (apart, of course, from the stale bread!) and the idiosyncrasies of individual cooks. Some less generous cooks use mostly onions and bread for panzanella, but it is best made with masses of very red and juicy tomatoes when they are at their ripest from June until the end of August. Don't be put off by the idea of stale bread in a salad, but do wring it out very well

8 ~ 10 PIECES HARD STALE BREAD
6 VERY RIPE TOMATOES, ROUGHLY CHOPPED
2 LARGE ONIONS, PREFERABLY RED ONIONS, SLICED THINLY
2 STICKS CELERY AND LEAVES, DICED
1 CUCUMBER CUT IN CHUNKS
8 OR MORE FRESH BASIL LEAVES, BRUISED IN A MORTAR
GOOD OLIVE OIL
SALT & PEPPER
RED WINE VINEGAR

Soak the bread in cold water for 15~20 minutes. Squeeze it out very well and crumble into a salad bowl. Add the vegetables, oil, basil, salt and pepper. Chill in the refrigerator for 2~3 hours. Just before serving toss with wine vinegar and some more basil if you have it.

45

SCHIACCIATA con L'UVA
Traditional flat cake
• with grapes •

Schiacciata means 'squashed flat' and this is a very ancient flat cake that has been made at the time of the vendemmia (grape harvest) in Tuscany since Etruscan times over 2000 years ago. It was devised, like so many dishes, as a method for using existing materials; left-over bread dough for the base and quantities of black wine grapes for the topping. If you are bothered by the seeds in Schiacciata you can make it with seedless grapes, or de-pip the grapes you are using, but it will not be as authentic, or as much fun - there won't be any pips to spit out, although a polite crunching sound is more usual in restaurants.

FOR THE BASE
1 LB 2 OZ/500 G PLAIN WHITE
   FLOUR, SIFTED
1 OZ/25 G FRESH YEAST
PINCH SALT
2½ OZ/60 G GRANULATED SUGAR
½ OZ/15 G ANISE SEED
   (SWEET CUMIN)
3/4 CUP WATER

FOR THE TOPPING
2 LB 2 OZ/1 KG LARGE JUICY
   BLACK GRAPES, WASHED
4 OZ/100 G CASTER SUGAR
SEVERAL SPRIGS FRESH ROSEMARY
6 ~ 8 TBSP OLIVE OIL

Warm the water and add the yeast, blend until smooth. On a pastry board or work-surface make a mound of the flour, salt and granulated sugar. Make a well in the middle and slowly pour in the yeast mixture, blending with a wooden spoon or spatula until smooth. When the yeast has been incorporated, knead the dough for 5~10 minutes as you would for bread. When it is smooth and elastic, cover and put in a warm room. When it has doubled in size, grease a rectangular baking tray (about 20" × 12"/51 × 30.5cm) with oil. Roll out the dough so that it is no more than ½"/1cm thick and 2"/5cm bigger all around than the tray. Place the dough on the tray and cover completely with the grapes. Sprinkle with the sugar and pour oil (in which you have heated the rosemary for

several minutes) over the top. Fold up the sides of the dough and pinch at the corners to make a rectangular shape. Bake for 30 minutes in an oven preheated to 350°F/175°C/Gas 4. It is best to put another pan underneath the Schiacciata as the juice from the grapes may overflow. Use these juices to baste the top of the cake. Chill in the refrigerator and just before serving drizzle it with honey.

There is another method for making Schiacciata con l'uva. At Spaltenna Anna makes the dough as above and then mixes into it the grapes and oil in which she has heated the rosemary and a cup of walnuts. She then rolls it out to no more than 1"/2.5cm and bakes it like a crusty flat bread or scone (at the same temperature). When the grapes are really lush, their juice stains the cake a deep crimson.

47

·FATTORIA·DI·MONTAGLIARI·

Giovanni Cappelli, the owner of the Fattoria di Montagliari, an excellent trattoria & vineyard near Panzano, is a faithful patron of the Antica Macelleria in Greve, (pages 50~51). His cook specializes in local Chiantigiana cuisine and Signor Cappelli himself is quite a culinary expert. These recipes are from his own handwritten collection. The Fattoria di Montagliari also has one of the largest vin santeries in Tuscany and produces one of the best vin santos. The Riserva 1968 is particularly fine.

· CROSTINI ROSSI ·

Piquant tomato crostini (4)

1 PIECE WHOLEWHEAT BREAD
1 CLOVE GARLIC
1 TBSP CAPERS
3 TBSP OLIVE OIL
COARSE SALT
FRESHLY GROUND BLACK PEPPER
WINE VINEGAR
3 TBSP FRESH PARSLEY
2 TBSP FRESH THYME
2 LARGE RIPE TOMATOES, PEELED
8 PIECES FRENCH BREAD OR
    DEEP FRIED POLENTA

Soak the wholewheat bread in vinegar and wring out well. Put in a mortar with the rest of the ingredients (except for the French bread) and pound to a rough paste. Chill and serve on toasted French bread or deep fried polenta (see recipe opposite)

· CECINA ·
Chickpea savoury bread (4)

9 OZ/250 G CHICKPEA FLOUR
    1 3/4 PT/1 LITRE WATER
    1/2 GLASS OLIVE OIL
    SALT

Sift the flour into a bowl, make a well in the middle and slowly add the water, beating well to avoid lumps forming. Add the oil and salt and blend in. Pour into a greased shallow baking tin to a depth of not more than 1/2 in/1 cm. Bake in an oven pre-heated to 450°F/ 230°C / Gas 8 until golden brown. Serve cut in wedges with plenty of freshly ground black pepper.

· SALSA di NOCI ·
Walnut sauce for pasta (6)

A recipe for pasta sauce that
Giovanni Cappelli believes
dates from at least the 1400s
in Siena. He serves it in his
restaurant with tortelli but
it is also very good with a
flat pasta like tagliatelle

7 OZ/200 G WALNUTS
2 OZ/50 G PINE NUTS
2 CLOVES GARLIC
3 BASIL LEAVES OR MORE
   ACCORDING TO TASTE
2 TBSP BREADCRUMBS
½ PT/300 ML MILK
   OR MORE ~ ENOUGH
   TO MAKE A SAUCE
   THE CONSISTENCY OF
   THICK CREAM
3 TBSP OLIVE OIL
SALT
PEPPER

   If you want to feel authen~
tically quattrocentoish, you
could pound all the above
ingredients together in a
mortar to make the sauce. A
food processor is faster, if
less romantic. Serve the sauce
over the pasta and then sprinkle
with whole walnuts and more
basil to make the dish espec~
ially good.

· POLENTA FRITTA ·
Deep fried polenta (4~6)

Polenta is a corn meal porridge
more popular in the north
than in Tuscany. Tuscan cooks
tend to prefer it first chilled
and then crisply deep-fried in
small golden wedges under
rich game sauces, or to replace
toast in antipasti.

7 OZ/200 G COARSE~GRAINED
   CORN MEAL
SALT
OIL FOR DEEP FRYING

Boil 2 pints of water in a
large saucepan, add salt and
lower heat. When
water is just sim~
mering begin to
add cornmeal,
pouring in a thin
stream, stirring
constantly with a
wooden spoon to
prevent lumps
forming. Continue
stirring for about
15~20 minutes after
all the cornmeal has been
added. The polenta is
cooked as soon as it begins to
stand away from the side of
the pan. Pour immediately
into a shallow baking tray
to a thickness of not more
than ½ in/1cm. Smooth out
any lumps and chill. When
cool enough to slice, cut into
diamond shapes that are
approximately 2½ in/5cm
long by 2in/4cm wide and
deep fry in hot oil a few at a
time. They are cooked when
transparent yellow and crusty
on both sides.

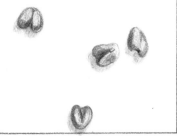

Just off the main square in Greve is the Antica Macelleria Falorni, a butcher's shop that every harassed din~ ner~party giver would like to live next to. This business, established in the 1840s, has become justifiably famous all over Italy for the quality of its meat. The proprietors, Lor~ enzo and Stefano Bencistà, proudly claim that every morning on opening there are at least 60 different cuts of meat for sale, as well as roasts, meatballs and Tuscan shishkebabs pre~ pared to their mother's recipes with fresh herbs, juniper berries, tomatoes & red peppers. Their acclaimed FINOCCHIONA sausage is made not with the usual cultivated fennel, but with feathery wild fennel gathered locally in the Chianti hills. And most astonishing of all, they still make, to an antique and ridiculously non~commercial recipe, prosciutto casalingo sotto cenere, now completely unavaible anywhere else. The ham is first stamped with the date, and then buried under wood ashes for up to two years. Origin~ ally the Tuscan peasants preserved their pork in this way throughout the summer months to have it, pink and tender, to eat dur~ ing the long cold winter. Lorenzo does it now, he says, not to make money, because its impossible to do on a large scale, but 'purely for the satisfaction of it, to keep the old traditions alive'. The Antica Macelleria Falorni also exports wild boar sausages and prosciutto all over Europe.

ARISTA di MAIALE
· ARROSTO ·
Roast loin of Pork (5~6)

If bistecca fiorentina is Tus~
cany's most famous meat
dish, this recipe comes a
close second. 'ARISTA' is the
Tuscan word for loin of pork,
and at the Falorni Macelleria
they cut the loin to keep long
bones on the chops. These are
then used as a kind of
natural grilling rack.
In some restaurants
Arista is made
with boned
pork with
not such a
tasty result
as this one.

4 ½ LB / 2 KG
   LOIN OF
   PORK
2 CLOVES OF
   GARLIC
OLIVE OIL
2 SPRIGS FRESH ROSEMARY
1 WINEGLASS WHITE WINE
SEA SALT
BLACK PEPPER, COARSELY GROUND

Finely chop the garlic and
rosemary together. With a sharp
knife make several cuts in the
pork near the bone and stuff
with the herbs. Lightly score
the outside of the meat and
rub plenty of salt, oil and
pepper into it to give a crispy
skin. Put the wine in a roast~
ing pan and then place the
meat resting on its bones in
the roasting pan (see drawing).
Cook in a moderate oven pre~
heated to 350°F/180°C/
Gas 4 for 1½~2 hours,
basting occasionally
with the
juices. Serve
with plain
boiled
canne~
lini beans
and a jug
of olive oil
to pour
over accor~
ding to taste. Or skim the fat
off the pan juices, simmer for
a few minutes with some
more wine and herbs and
pour the resulting sauce over
the beans instead of using
olive oil.

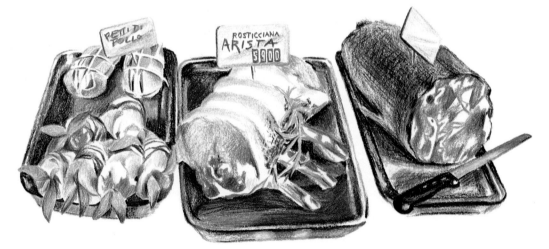

· STUFATINO di VITELLO ·
Tuscan veal stew (4~6)

1 ½ LB/700 G LEAN VEAL, CUT
    IN CUBES
1 WINE GLASS WHITE WINE (APPROX)
OLIVE OIL
SALT
PEPPER
¼ CHILI PEPPER, FINELY CHOPPED
1~2 LARGE RIPE TOMATOES,
    PEELED, SEEDED & CHOPPED
    OR 3 TBSP TOMATO PUREE IF
    TOMATOES ARE NOT TASTY
2 CLOVES GARLIC, CRUSHED
3 TBSP CHOPPED PARSLEY
FLOUR

Brown the garlic and chili
pepper in oil in a heavy casse~
role. Add the veal, well dusted
with flour, and let it brown.
Pour in the wine and when
nearly evaporated, add the
tomatoes or the tomato
puree. Season to taste, lower
the heat and cook covered
until the meat is tender,
about 1 hour. Stir in the
parsley just before serving. It
is delicious served with deep~
fried polenta and fagioli
all'uccelletto. A thinly
sliced fennel bulb added 10
minutes before the end of
cooking makes an excellent
addition to the classic version
of the dish.

· POLPETTINI ·
Tuscan meatballs (6)

Every country has its version
of the meatball. In Tuscany
they're called POLPETTINI if
they're small. When, as often
happens, they are almost the
size of a meat loaf, they are

called POLPETTONE. At the
Locanda dell'Amorosa near
Siena they serve tiny spicy
polpettini, crunchily deep-
fried, as a hot appetizer in the
winter months.

1 LB 2 OZ/500G COOKED PORK OR
   BEEF, CUT IN CUBES
3 OZ/75 G GRATED PARMESAN OR
   PECORINO
4 OZ/100 G PROSCIUTTO (OR HAM)
2 POTATOES, PEELED AND COOKED
2 EGGS, BEATEN
2 CLOVES GARLIC, CRUSHED
HANDFUL PARSLEY, CHOPPED
4 SAGE LEAVES, CHOPPED
JUICE OF 1 LEMON
SALT
PEPPER
½ TSP NUTMEG
(OPTIONAL ¼ TSP CINNAMON)
OIL FOR DEEP FRYING

Put the meat and potatoes
through a fine grinder, mincer
or food processor and then mix
well with other ingredients.
Form tiny round meatballs of
a maximum 1 in/2.5 cm diameter and roll in cornmeal or,
better still, breadcrumbs.
Deep fry a few at a time in
oil until crunchy and golden
brown. Drain well and serve
hot with a selection of other
antipasti.

53

· LOCANDA · GIOVANNI ·

Go into the Antica Macelleria first thing in the morning and you are likely to run into half the cooks and restaurant~owners in the area. Rossella Rossi, proprietress of the Locanda Giovanni da Verrazzano in Greve does her shopping there and, with the Bencista brothers' excellent lean veal, makes this unusual version of a classic Tuscan dish. This recipe for Stracotto, meaning overcooked, comes from an old Florentine cookbook and supposedly dates from the sixteenth century.

STRACOTTO al CHIANTI CLASSICO
· Beef with red wine (6) ·

4 ½ LB / 2 KG BONED FILLET OF
    VEAL OR BONED TOP RUMP
    OF BEEF.
3 OZ / 75 G PINE NUTS
3 OZ / 75 G RAISINS
3 OZ / 75 G PEELED TOASTED ALMONDS
½ HOT CHILI PEPPER, CHOPPED
1 ONION, FINELY CHOPPED
1 CARROT, FINELY CHOPPED
1 BOTTLE CHIANTI CLASSICO
2 CLOVES GARLIC
HANDFUL FRESH PARSLEY
1 PINT GOOD BEEF STOCK
SALT & PEPPER

DA · VERRAZZANO ·

Soften the onion, chili pepper & carrot in oil in a deep casser~ole. Meanwhile chop the nuts, raisins, garlic and parsley roughly. With a small sharp knife make cuts in several places all over the meat and stuff with half the nut mix~ture. Tie into a neat shape with string and brown on all sides in the casserole. Pour in the wine, add remaining nut mixture and top up with stock so the meat is just cov~ered. Simmer covered for at least 2¼ hours, or untill meat is tender, adding more stock to keep the meat cov~ered. Remove the string, slice meat thinly and keep warm. Reduce the sauce and serve over meat, making sure some of the nuts and raisins are included. This is a won~derfully rich tasting dish that is best served with something simple such as plain buttered pasta or crisp greens.

· RISTORANTE · IL · FEDINO ·

In the busy town of San Casciano in Val di Pesa, the locals have their own spec~ ial gathering place ~ the Ristorante Il Fedino, a 15th-century villa on the road to Florence. The proprietor serves essentially rustic dishes in the cool wine cellars below the family home.

CONIGLIO RIPIENO
· Stuffed Rabbit (6) ·

This way of cooking rabbit is the speciality at Il Fedino. You can use frozen rabbit from the supermarket, but the flavour will not be as good as when wild rabbit is used.

1	LARGE RABBIT, CLEANED, BONED AND FLATTENED
2	EGGS
6	TBSP GRATED PECORINO OR PARMESAN CHEESE
1/2	TSP GRATED NUTMEG
	SEVERAL SPRIGS FRESH THYME
8 FL OZ/225 ML	BEEF STOCK
	OLIVE OIL
	BUTTER
	COARSE SEA SALT
	PEPPER

Get your butcher or game deal~ er to clean and bone the rab~ bit ~ it is not an easy task for the unskilled. Beat the eggs with the salt and pepper and cook in butter to make a thin omelette. Lay the rabbit out flat and put the omelette on it. Dot with but~ ter and sprin~ kle on the pecorino, nutmeg & thyme. Roll the rabbit up and tie it carefully, having tucked the ends in.

Rub plenty of pepper and coarse sea salt into the rab~ bit. Heat a few table~ spoons of olive oil in a shallow flame~proof casserole and brown the rabbit on all sides in it. Reduce the heat & add the stock, cover. Continue cook~ ing for 1½ hours, adding more stock if necessary. When tender, remove the string and serve sliced very thinly in the pan juices with more fresh thyme stripped over the top.

56

FEGATELLI di MAIALE

Tuscan pork liver
• bruschettes (4) •

A classic Tuscan dish cooked either in a frying pan or grilled, as in these two recipes, over charcoal. At Pedino's they vary the recipe slightly by chop~ ~ping & pre~cooking the liver before gril~ ling, which guar~ antees its tenderness ~ this is given as the second version of the recipe.

4 AROMATIC TWIGS (IE: BAY, ROSEMARY ETC.) FROM WHICH THE LEAVES HAVE BEEN STRIPPED
1 LB 2 OZ / 500 G PORK LIVER
1 TBSP FENNEL SEEDS
4 TBSP BREADCRUMBS OR 4 PIECES BREAD, CUT IN CHUNKS
OLIVE OIL
ABOUT 1 LB / 450 G CAUL FAT ✱ OR BACON
HANDFUL FRESH SAGE OR BAY LEAVES
SALT & PEPPER

• METHOD I •

Crush the fennel seeds in a mortar with the salt & pepper. Soak the caul fat in water to soften. Cut into squares approx~ imately 4 x 4 in / 10 x 10 cm. Cut the liver into bite size chunks and roll in the fennel. Then wrap each piece in caul and skewer on a twig, alternating the liver with a sage or bay leaf and a chunk of bread dipped in olive oil. Cook over fire for 15 ~ 20 minutes or until caul fat is crisp.

• METHOD II •

Crush the fennel seeds with the salt and pepper, breadcrumbs and 3 sage leaves. Chop liver into small pieces and cook until slight~ ly browned. Mix with other ingre~ dients, wrap in fat and then in a sage or bay leaf. (If using dried bay leaves soak them well first.) Skewer & grill for 10 minutes or until caul fat is crisp.

✱ CAUL FAT or PORK NET (obtainable from butchers in ethnic neighbourhoods) is a lacy fat from the pig's intestines. If you cannot get it or are squeam~ ish, wrap the liver in bacon instead. The fat, however, does add a remarkably flavourful juice to the liver and keeps it very moist.

• PINZIMINIO •
Olive~oil dip

At the CASTELLARE estate near Castel~
lina in Chianti, the olive oil is sold in
lovely square glass decanters and the
wines and olive oils are distinguished by
painted labels of local Chiantigiana birds.

The best way to test the flavour of a
good olive oil is to make Pinziminio, nothing
more than oil into which generous amounts
of coarse sea salt and black pepper have
been ground. Tuscans use it as a dip for
fresh or briefly scalded vegetables such
as fennel root, artichokes, red peppers
and asparagus.

MEDIEVAL CITIES

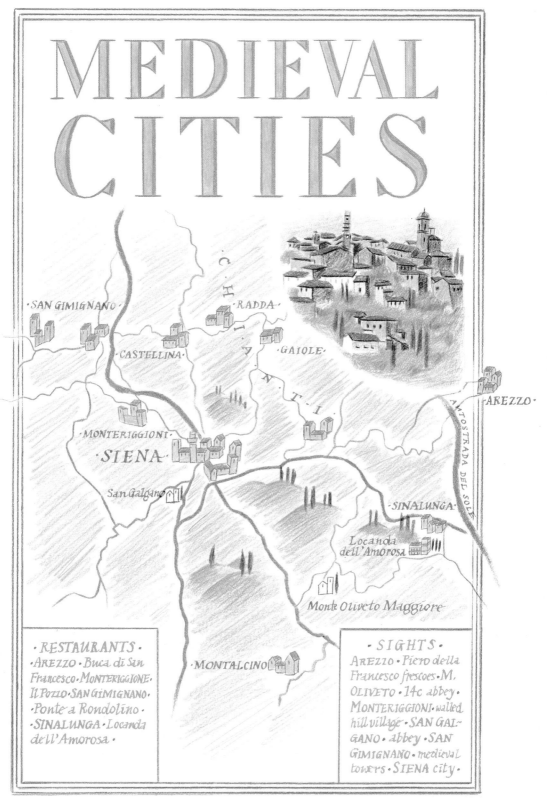

· SAN GIMIGNANO ·

· RADDA ·

· CASTELLINA ·

· GAIOLE ·

C H I A N T I

· AREZZO ·

AUTOSTRADA DEL SOLE

· MONTERIGGIONI ·

· SIENA ·

San Galgano

· SINALUNGA ·

Locanda dell'Amorosa

Monte Oliveto Maggiore

· RESTAURANTS ·
· AREZZO · Buca di San
Francesco · MONTERIGGIONE ·
Il Pozzo · SAN GIMIGNANO ·
· Ponte a Rondolino ·
· SINALUNGA · Locanda
dell'Amorosa ·

· MONTALCINO ·

· SIGHTS ·
AREZZO · Piero della
Francesco frescoes · M.
OLIVETO · 14c abbey ·
MONTERIGGIONI · walled
hill village · SAN GAL-
GANO · abbey · SAN
GIMIGNANO · medieval
towers · SIENA city ·

· INTRODUCTION ·

The story goes that Senius and Aschio, sons of Remus, fled Rome in search of peace and founded a castle in Tuscany that became Siena. There is little remaining Roman influence today apart from the wolf symbol that is prominent in the city's emblems. Siena is a city of Gothic art and architecture, built of red~gold 'burnt Siena' bricks and surrounded by what Virginia Woolf called 'the loveliest of all land~scapes'. It is famous for the beauty and clarity of its language, for its rich oriental~tasting sweets like panforte and ricciarelli and for the Palio, a bare~backed horse race of medieval origins that provides a year~long undercurrent of tension to an other~wise gentle, dreamy city.

The city's past is not a peaceful one. For hundreds of years Ghibelline Siena was the sworn and violent enemy of Guelf Florence. In nearby medieval and Renaissance towns like San Gimignano, Monteriggioni, Montepulciano and Montalcino constant battles were fought between the two city~states. Siena's greatest victory came in 1260 with the defeat of Florence at the battle of Montaperti. Still celebrated today as a glorious event, the battle is less significant than the overwhelming Florentine victory nine years later. This victory, although galling for the Sienese, and in the long run destroying their prosperity, was initially the start of a 'Golden Age' for Siena.

In 1287 'Nine Good Men' chosen from the mid~dle classes to rule the city were responsible for a seventy~year period of great prosperity and art~istic achievement. Most of the work on Siena's magnificent Duomo, begun in the late twelfth century, was completed during this time, including the astonishing black and white striped mosque~like interior. Even more successful was the development of Siena's central square, the Campo, into one of the most magical city centres in Italy. Entered through narrow, covered archways, the square slopes inwards like the hub of a giant wheel. The mellow brick paving is divided into nine spokes symbolizing the Nine Good Men responsible and at the centre is the elegant and much-copied Palazzo Pubblico. Its graceful bell-tower of 503 steps soars into the air over the Campo's fourteenth-century palaces. During the build-up to the Palio, the bell rings methodically and rythmically like the city's heart-beat until minutes before the race begins.

It could be said that the Palio itself is the city's heartbeat, and to understand the Palio is to understand Siena. Briefly it is this: a race three times around the Campo in which ten jockeys ride bareback horses representing the ten contrade (city wards) competing in the race. There are seventeen wards in all, each one a sworn enemy of the other, but for safety's sake not all compete. The only official prize is a silk banner called the 'Palio', and the race for it lasts roughly a minute. But this minute is the culmination of a whole year's hopes and preparation, of a final three day's feasting, parades and sometimes violent fights between rival contrade. At the end of this minute the winning contrada will go, quite

SIENA

1000

Serie III.

10 CARTOLINE - VEDUTE DELLA CITTÀ

62

simply, mad with joy; laughing, crying, singing and marching the streets of Siena all night carrying the Palio banner. It is entirely medieval, unlike any other spectacle in the world. People faint from heat and excitement. Jockeys are thrown into the barriers and killed. Horses, drugged before the race, roll over, crash into one another, break legs and are shot. It has been criticized for its barbarity and it is barbaric without a doubt. But no one who has seen it, who has stood inside a church before the race and watched a priest bless a horse, listened to his strange cry 'Vai cavallino e torna vincatore!' (Go little horse and return a winner!) and to the haunting accompanying canto of the surrounding people; who has watched the two hour medieval parade through the streets or the river of people that floods the race square up to the last possible minute; who has seen the old and wily horse Panezio, winner of an astonishing eight Palios, thread his nimble way through the pack of careening jockeys and riderless horses, around the virtually right-angled corner of the campo that is the most dangerous, or who has heard the spine-tingling cry 'Daccelo' (Give it to us!) after the victory, can fail to be moved by the Palio. To say that it is just a horserace is like saying that Everest is just a mountain. The Palio is not an event that occurs twice a year at Siena. It _is_ Siena.

The only place to eat in Siena is in the street the night before the Palio. Each of the city's wards has a traditional dinner, with tables a quarter of a mile long laid for 200 and 300 people. The jockeys are there, feted and kissed by beautiful girls. Siena's nobility sit next to the local barbers. There are speeches and songs, and somehow miraculously in the middle of all this the food arrives, hot and good, for those who are not too excited to eat it. If you cannot beg, borrow or steal a ticket to one of these meals, there are still plenty of restaurants that push their tables into the street and serve up the Palio atmosphere as well as food.

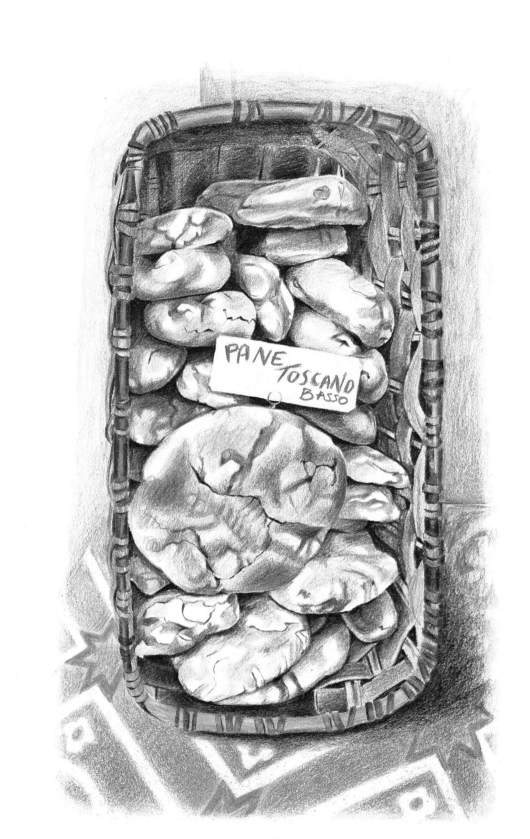

Bread is the pasta of Tuscany. It is used far more than flour or pasta to thicken soups & stews & give textures to sauces. A good Tuscan 'pan basso' loaf has almost no salt & when stale it tends to go hard & dry rather than moldy, thus remaining useful for cooking. At A. Sclavi's Panificio Moderno the bread variations are endless, all displayed in old wicker baskets around the shop. And the fresh pasta is so good that the Locanda dell'Amorosa restaurant near Sinalunga used to send a bus to Siena every weekend to collect a fresh batch.

· PANE BASSO ·
Tuscan country bread (2 loaves)

At the Panificio Moderno the baker uses brewer's yeast in the bread but this recipe using fresh yeast gives a similar result. You can make Pane integrale, the closest the Tuscans get to wholewheat bread, by substituting 1/4 lb/100g bran for the same quantity of white flour in the following recipe.

2 OZ/50G FRESH YEAST
1 PT/500 ML WARM WATER (LUKEWARM)
2 LB/900 G STRONG WHITE FLOUR

Dissolve the yeast in 3 fl oz/175 ml of the warm water in a small bowl. Sift in enough of the flour to make a soft dough, mixing with the hands. Cover & put in a warm place to rise. When the yeast dough has at least doubled in size, begin making the rest of the dough. Sift the remaining flour onto a wood or marble surface. Make a well in the middle, pour a little water into it & begin working the flour towards this with your hands. When the dough has absorbed enough water to bind together, add the yeast dough and work in. Knead for 5~10 minutes, occasionally lifting the dough & smacking it on the table. Continue until it no longer sticks to your hands. Sprinkle a large bowl with water and put the dough in it. Cover with a cloth & let rise in a warm place until doubled in size (about 30 minutes). Knead again 5~10 minutes and form into 2 balls. Let stand another 20 minutes and then bake on a greased, floured baking tin until crusty (about 30 minutes) in an oven preheated to 350°F/180°C Gas 4.

PAN coSANTI

PANE francese casalingo

65

PANFORTE di SIENA
· Traditional Siena ·
— spice cake —

5 OZ / 150 G SUGAR (GRANULATED)
7 OZ / 200 G ALMONDS, PEELED
7 OZ / 200 G WALNUTS, CLEANED
11 OZ / 300 G MIXED CANDIED
   FRUIT, CHOPPED
4 OZ / 100 G HONEY
4 OZ / 100 G DRIED FIGS
2½ OZ / 60 G COCOA
   POWDER
¼ TSP POWDERED
   CORIANDER
¼ TSP POWDERED
   CLOVES
½ TSP POWDERED
   NUTMEG
¼ TSP WHITE PEPPER
¾ TSP CINNAMON
2 OZ / 50 G FLOUR
10 LARGE BAKING WAFERS OR
   RICE PAPER

The history of Panforte or 'strong bread' dates back as far as, or further, than Siena itself and there are many recipes for it, some of which seem almost too spicey for modern palates. When panforte was first made this over~spicing probably served to preserve, as well as to cover the unwelcome taste of mold. Today the brightly~wrapped Panforte cakes in Siena are as much a part of the city as the Palio. Made before Christmas and stored in an air~tight container, the cake will keep for about a month. Served in thin slices with strong black coffee it makes an interesting alternative to christmas cake. In Siena it is often topped with melted dark chocolate instead of the icing sugar used in this recipe.

Toast the nuts in a hot oven and chop roughly. Put in a bowl with all the dried fruit, spices and cocoa. Sift in the flour and mix well. In a double saucepan or a basin over a pan of boiling water, boil the honey carefully & melt in the sugar. Stir constantly until it will form a soft ball between your fingers (remember to dip your fingers in cold water before testing for this). Immediately pour onto the fruit and blend in well with your hands. Firm the dough into a flat round cake about 1 in / 2.5 cm

QUARESIMALI
£ 2500 l'etto

PANFORTE a taglio £ 2000 l'etto

Crush the almonds to a powder in a mortar, or put through a nut-grinder, making sure you don't lose any of the oil. Mix well with the caster sugar and rub through a sieve into a large bowl. Whip the egg whites to form soft peaks. Fold into the almond/caster sugar mixture together with the icing sugar and orange peel. It should make a soft, smooth paste. Form into diamond-shaped lozenges, each lozenge about ½ in/1cm thick, 2 in/4.5 cm long and 1½ in/3.5 cm wide. Dust heavily with more icing sugar, place each lozenge on a piece of rice paper and leave for 12 hours. Bake in an oven so low that it is just warm (275°F/140°C/Gas 1) for about 15 minutes. Cool on a wire rack and serve with more icing sugar sifted on top. It is always a good idea to use vanilla sugar for this (sugar stored with a vanilla pod).

thick. Lay the wafers on a buttered baking sheet and place the cake on top. Bake for 40 minutes, until dry, in an oven preheated to 350°F/180°C/Gas 4. When cool trim wafers to fit the cake and dust the top of the cake with a mixture of icing sugar and cinnamon.

· RICCIARELLI ·
Sweet almond biscuits (2 dozen)

These sweet and wickedly rich macaroons are almost as famous in Siena as panforte. They have the taste of oriental sweetmeats about them and are costly to make and buy, even in Siena. If you buy your ricciarelli at A. Sclavi's they will wrap them, however few, with ribbon and pretty paper, as if they were precious Christmas gifts.

12 ¼ OZ/360 G PEELED ALMONDS
6 OZ/180 G ICING SUGAR, SIFTED
8 ¾ OZ/240 G CASTER SUGAR, SIFTED
1 TBSP GRATED ORANGE PEEL
2 EGG WHITES
2 DOZEN ROUNDS RICE PAPER

Seen from the valley below, San Gimignano lives up to its reputation as a medieval Manhattan. Fifteen stone towers rise above the ochre~coloured walls, the last reminders of how all towns in Tuscany looked 600 years ago. In 1300, when Dante visited San Gimignano as ambassador, there were 72 towers, all built as keeps during the struggles between two warring families, the Ardinghelli and the Salvucci. Over centuries of feuding the towers were destroyed one by one until today only the fifteen remain, their crevices rootholds for straggling wild capers.

Politics may be less violent and towers may have fallen, but San Gimignano has kept its medieval appearance and apart from the growing collection of tourist shops, is virtually unchanged since the fourteenth century. In the Piazza della Cisterna, water flows from a thirteenth~century cistern and the cobbled square is sur~ rounded by houses built in the golden limestone of that region. One of the towers dominates the Piazza del Poppolo and once a week the timeless bustle of a street market fills the Piazza del Duomo.

· SALSA ·
per la CACCIA-GIONE
Hunter's Sauce

In San Gimignano's market you can find everything from the local hand~painted blue and white china to ravioli rolling pins and homemade pasta. Or buy a hot courgette flower fritter and a fresh bread roll filled with roast wild boar that has been basted in a sauce such as this.

2 CLOVES GARLIC, CRUSHED
OLIVE OIL
1 TBSP CAPERS
7~8 SAGE LEAVES, CHOPPED
LEAVES FROM 1 STALK ROSEMARY,
     CHOPPED FINELY
2 WINEGLASSES RED WINE
1 ANCHOVY FILLET, MASHED

Fry the garlic in the oil until golden. Add capers, sage and rosemary and cook for a minute or two. Pour in the red wine and bring to the boil. When slightly reduced, stir in the an~ chovy and use to baste any barbecued game from rabbit, or pigeon to pheasant. It is also excellent with roast pork. When the meat is cooked, spoon any remaining sauce over it and serve hot.

· FIORI FRITTI ·
Courgette flower fritters (6)

Freshly picked courgette flowers are a delicacy usually available only to people fortunate enough to have their own vegetable gardens. In Tuscany, however, the huge orange and green blossoms are available through~ out the summer in most markets.

(continued on next page)

16~18 COURGETTE (ZUCCHINI) FLOWERS
SMALL HANDFUL FRESH HERBS (PARSLEY
AND/OR THYME) FINELY CHOPPED
3¾ OZ/96 G PLAIN WHITE FLOUR
½ PT/300 ML COLD WATER
SALT & PEPPER
OIL FOR DEEP FRYING

Gently wash & dry the flowers. Trim off stems. In a bowl slowly sift the flour into the water, beating well with a wooden spoon until the mixture is like a smooth pancake batter. Mix in the herbs. Heat the oil in a deep pan and when very hot, dip the blossoms quickly into the batter & then into the oil. When they are golden brown drain on a kitchen towel & sprinkle with salt and pepper. Serve immediately while still hot. In Tuscany this method is used to cook many different flowers and leaves, such as clematis and borage.

· FIORI con RIPIENO ·
Stuffed zucchini flowers (6)

For a more filling version of the fritters the flowers can be filled with a savoury stuffing.

6 OZ/175 G GRATED
PARMESAN
2 OZ/60 G HAM OR BACON
CHOPPED
1 CLOVE GARLIC, CRUSHED
2 TBSF PARSLEY, FINELY CHOPPED
3 OZ/75 G FINE BREADCRUMBS
SALT & FRESHLY GROUND BLACK PEPPER
1 BEATEN EGG
2 TBSF MILK

Mix all the ingredients together. Spoon the mixture carefully into the flowers, tucking over the petal tops so it won't escape, then follow the previous recipe for simple flower fritters. Serve hot.

For July, in Siena, by the willow tree, I give you barrels of white Tuscan wine...

(SAN GIMIGNANO FOLKLORE)

And that most Tuscan of Tuscan white wines ~ Vernaccia di San Gimignano is as much a part of San Gimignano as its towers. Rep~ utedly favoured by Dante it is now sold in shops & cantinas all over the town. Some vineyards, such as Fattoria di Cusano, Raccianello & Pietrafitta, are open to the public. Enrico Teruzzi's Ponte a Rondolino vineyard serves one of the best vernaccias at its own excellent trattoria just outside town.

RISOTTO alla VERNACCIA
· Risotto with white wine (6) ·

Of the several risotto recipes in this book, this is the plainest & most delicate & therefore the most easy to make badly. The rice must be Italian Arborio rice for the proper outer creaminess & inner firmness & both the stock & the wine must be of good quality. For preference use Vernaccia, a vigorous tasting white wine, but if it is not available,

use a similarly strong flavoured white wine. Be lavish, the risotto should taste of wine, not water.

1 MEDIUM ONION, FINELY CHOPPED
1½ OZ/40 G BUTTER
12 OZ/350 G ITALIAN ARBORIO RICE
1½ PTS/900 ML CHICKEN STOCK (APPROX)
6 FL OZ/175 ML VERNACCIA (OR MORE)

Melt the butter in a medium~ sized pan. Saute the onion until a pale brown and then add the rice, stirring until glistening & semi~transparent. Meanwhile heat the stock in a saucepan. Turn up the heat under the rice and pour in the wine, when it has almost disappeared add about ½ pt/300 ml hot stock and, when absorbed, add a similar amount. Continue to add more stock (or wine for a stronger fla~ vour) a spoonful at a time as it is absorbed by the rice (the rice will become noticeably flat on top when it needs more liquid). It should take about 20~30 minutes to cook. Stir frequently while ad~ ding liquid & just before serving stir in some butter & several tablespoons of grated pecorino or parmesan cheese.

The best Sienese food is served not in Siena but half an hour's drive away near the old town of Sinalunga. A long straight line of spiky black cypresses leads up a hill to a brick archway, the entrance to the Locanda dell'Amorosa, the 'lover's' inn. It is less a hotel and restaurant than a small village, the heart of a busy farm estate or 'fattoria' producing its own Chianti colli Senesi (chianti from the Sienese hills) as well as olive oil, home made marmelades, jams and honeys.

In Siena's Museo Civico there is a fresco showing the farm as it was in 1300, but it could hardly have been a more beautiful or magical place then than it is now. The res~ taurant, built into the old stables, looks out on a peaceful central courtyard of the 1400s where roses climb over mellow pink bricks. The menu changes to suit each season and is skilfully supervised by the shy and dedicated Guiseppe Vacarini, who is also one of the best sommeliers in Italy. The owner, Carlo Citterio, whose fam~ ily has lived and worked at

L'Amorosa
for generations,
is completely enam-
oured of his home, as are
all his staff. It shows.
It is possible to arrive at
l'Amorosa, tired and har-
assed, with half of Tuscany's
considerable insect population stuck to your car's
windshield and to leave
there (though unwillingly)
two hours later appetite
satisfied and spirits restored completely.

·LOCANDA dell'AMOROSA·

The food at the Locanda dell' Amorosa can be as simple as a plate of fresh raw porcini mushrooms sliced paper thin and marinated in local oil and garden herbs, or rabbit simmered slowly in wine with the subtle taste of wild fennel seeds. In season there is the elegance of grilled quail and pheasant from the Sienese hills, or more traditional and substantial recipes like these two, excellent for cold days in late autumn when the first frost is on the ground.

· STRISCE con CECI ·
Ribbon noodles & chickpea soup (4)

STRISCE are wide ribbon noodles ideal for this thick soup that is more like noodles with a chickpea sauce.

---

14 oz / 400 G DRIED CHICK PEAS
  (SOAKED FOR 10 HRS, WATER DISCARDED)
4 oz / 100 G CARROTS, FINELY CHOPPED
1 SMALL ONION, FINELY CHOPPED
1 STICK CELERY, FINELY CHOPPED
4 TBSP OLIVE OIL
3 CLOVES GARLIC, PEELED
1 SPRIG ROSEMARY OR 2 TSP CHOPPED
  DRIED ROSEMARY
5 BLACK PEPPERCORNS
SALT
STRISCE OR MACCHERONI FOR 4~5
  (PASTA RECIPE PAGE 76)
  OR 250 G COMMERCIAL PASTA

Put the chickpeas in a deep saucepan with the garlic and pepper. Add enough water to cover plus one inch. Cover and cook slowly on a low heat for 3 hours. When tender remove the chickpeas, saving the liquid, and put all but 6 tablespoons of the chickpeas through a food processor or vegetable mill with the garlic. Heat the oil in a large saucepan and saute the carrots, onion, celery and rosemary until softened. Put everything, including the remaining chickpea liquid, into a saucepan & cook for another 30 minutes. Add salt to taste & the pasta & cook until just tender. Serve hot with grated parmesan.

· BOLLITO in SALSA ·
di DRAGONCELLO
Boiled beef & tarragon sauce (4)

Except for the Siena area tarragon is not commonly used in Tuscany. When it does appear it's often raw, rather than cooked in the French method. At the Locanda dell'Amorosa fresh tarragon for this recipe is grown in their old walled herb garden on a hill overlooking the surrounding vineyards.

· SAUCE ·

3 oz / 80 G FRESH BREADCRUMBS
1 oz / 20 G FRESH TARRAGON
1 TBSP WHITE WINE VINEGAR
5 TBSP OLIVE OIL
3 CLOVES GARLIC
SALT

· BOLLITO ·

14 oz / 400 G FATTY BEEF BRISKET,
  RUMP OR CHUCK STEAK
14 oz / 400 G BONED SHOULDER OF
  VEAL OR BEEF IN ONE PIECE
1 CARROT
1 SMALL ONION
1 CELERY STICK
1 TBSP CHOPPED PARSLEY
1 TSP SEA SALT

Put 3 litres of water into a deep saucepan with the vegetables, salt & parsley & bring to the boil. Add the meat & simmer slowly for 3 hours. Skim off any scum that rises to the surface. In the meantime make the sauce. Soak the breadcrumbs in vinegar for 15 minutes & squeeze out. Crush the tarragon & garlic to a paste in a mortar & rub through a sieve with the breadcrumbs. Mix well & slowly beat in the olive oil to obtain a thick smooth sauce. Salt to taste. When the beef is cooked slice it thinly, pour several ladles of broth over it & serve it with the tarragon sauce on the side.

· P A S T A ·

Commercial pasta bears little resemblance to the homemade variety, apart from a similar shape. Where pasta 'asciutta' (dry pasta available in packets) is only a vehicle for its sauce, homemade pasta is good enough to be an end in itself. The main difference is that the homemade varieties are made with fresh eggs and obviously worked by hand instead of machine. But many things can affect the quality of even an expert cook's pasta. Onelia, the pasta cook at the Locanda dell'Amorosa, cannot achieve the same degree of tenderness when making pasta dough at l'Amorosa as she can using the same technique in the Chianti district. One reason is the difference in water. Another is that many of the eggs in Chianti have very large yolks which absorb more flour. And as every good pasta cook knows, the more flour used, the firmer the dough and the firmer the dough, the better the pasta. Unfortunately for the novice, it is more difficult to work a very stiff dough.

· RAVIOLI con SPINACI ·
— Ravioli stuffed with — spinach & ricotta (6)

Although pasta is not as much a speciality in Tuscany as it is in Emilia~Romagna, it is still very popular. This recipe is one of the best Tuscan ways of serving fresh pasta, but the same ingredients for the dough may also be used to produce tagliatelle or pappardelle.

PASTA INGREDIENTS:
11~13 oz / 300~375 g PLAIN
    UNBLEACHED FLOUR
3 EGGS
PINCH OF SALT

STUFFING:
2½ LB / 1.2 KG FRESH SPINACH
    (OR NETTLES) WASHED WELL
½ TSP SALT
½ TSP NUTMEG
2 EGG YOLKS
12 OZ / 350 G RICOTTA CHEESE

1 First make the stuffing. Wash the spinach and put it into a saucepan with just the water that clings to the leaves. Add the salt. Cover and cook for 15~20 minutes, until tender. Drain, squeeze out moisture and chop very finely. Mix together with the other ingredients & salt to taste.

2 To make the pasta sift the flour with the salt on to a wooden table. Make a well in the middle of the flour and pour in the yolks, beaten lightly together with a fork. With your hand start stirring in flour from inside the well until the eggs are no longer liquid, and continue to work in until the eggs have absorbed as much flour as possible without losing pliability.

3 Wash your hands, clean the work surface of flour & knead the dough for about 10 minutes until it is a shiny flexible ball. Fold it over and turn it continuously as you knead it. Leave, covered, for about 10 minutes.

4 At this point you can use a pasta machine to do the final rolling out. Otherwise divide dough in two to make it easier to handle. Always keep unused dough covered. Rub some oil into a long thin rolling pin (24~30 in/60~75 cm long and 2 in/5 cm diameter is a good size) & then dust with flour. On a floured surface begin to roll the dough out as quickly as possible into a regular oval shape. Roll it smoothly away from you & turn it after each roll. As it gets thinner, occasionally wrap the sheet of pasta around a rolling pin and stretch towards you. When paper thin, fold loosely, cover & repeat the process with the other half.

5 Lay one sheet on a floured surface, cut into an even rectangular shape & place small teaspoonfuls of spinach filling approximately 1½ in/4 cm apart in straight rows. Between rows brush water, lay the other sheet of dough on top & with the side of the hand press firmly down between rows to seal. Cut into squares with a pastry cutter and place on greaseproof paper. Cover.

(Continued on following page)

(Continued from preceding page)

6 Boil 8 pints/4.5 litres of water with 1 tbsp oil & a tsp of salt. Add the pasta and about 5 minutes after the water has returned to the boil remove the ravioli, which should be cooked al dente. Serve immediately with butter and grated cheese or with butter in which you have fried 6~8 leaves of sage.

RAVIOLI GNUDI
Naked Ravioli (6)

There is another type of so-called 'ravioli' that is particularly popular in Tuscany although almost unavailable in any restaurants there. It is a bit like the stuffing without the pasta and in fact is called 'Ravioli gnudi' in Arezzo to indicate 'naked' ravioli. It is a great delicacy, good enough to eat with just freshly chopped tomatoes and a sprinkling of parmesan on top.

1½ LB/675G FRESH SPINACH, COOKED AS PREVIOUS RECIPE & FINELY CHOPPED
9 OZ/250 G RICOTTA CHEESE
4½ OZ/130 G PLAIN FLOUR
3 EGG YOLKS
5 OZ/150 G FRESHLY GRATED PECORINO OR PARMESAN
½ TSP NUTMEG
½ SMALL ONION, FINELY CHOPPED
2 OZ/50 G BUTTER
SALT

Melt the butter in a large saucepan. Cook the onion in it until golden. Add the spinach and salt and saute for about 5 minutes. Cool slightly and then in a large bowl mix together thoroughly with the ricotta and flour. Add the yolks, nutmeg and pecorino and work together well. Salt to taste. Chill well for easier handling and then form into oval pellets about 1 in/2.5 cm long by ½ in/1cm across. Boil 8 pints/4.5 litres salted water and cook the ravioli a few at a time. They should be ready about 3 or 4 minutes after the water has returned to the boil. Remove and keep warm until ready to eat. In the unlikely occurrence of leftovers, roll them in egg yolk and breadcrumbs the next day and deep fry until crunchy and brown.

BUCA DI SAN FRANCESCO

Arezzo is a prosperous, rather austere provincial town, the centre of a rich farming zone. It is internationally famous for the stunning frescoes there by Piero della Francesco but locally more famous for Mario de Filippis' friendly little trattoria, Buca di San Francesco. There you can sit in the frescoed cellar of a sixteenth-century palace and eat specialities such as zuppa di fagioli (bean soup), home-made tagliolini, ricotta with acacia honey, and chicken from the nearby Valdarno cooked 'in porchetta'. Porchetta is a whole roast piglet usually sold from stalls by travelling vendors throughout Tuscany and Umbria. Chicken cooked in the same way is stuffed with quantities of leafy wild fennel, sage leaves and garlic.

SFORMATO di VERDURE con FEGATINI
· Spinach souffle with · chicken livers (4)

Buca di San Francesco is one of a group of restaurants 'del Buon Ricordo' (good memory), established to keep alive the traditions of regional cooking in Italy. Each one has a dish, like this one, particularly typical of the area, called the 'Piatto del Buon Ricordo', and a regional menu that the restaurant's owner will recommend on request. This recipe uses spinach for the sformato, but is equally good made with nettles or swiss chard.

· SFORMATO ·

2 lb 2 oz / 1 kg SPINACH
3 fl oz / 75 ml THICK BECHAMEL
3 EGG WHITES, BEATEN STIFFLY
1 EGG YOLK, BEATEN
1/4 ~ 1/2 TSP NUTMEG
2 1/2 TBSP PARMESAN
2 oz / 50 g BUTTER
4 oz / 100 g FINE, DRY BREADCRUMBS
SALT & FRESHLY GROUND PEPPER

· SAUCE ·

1 LB/450 G CHICKEN LIVERS, TRIMMED OF FAT & WASHED
1 SMALL ONION, FINELY CHOPPED
4~6 TBSP OLIVE OIL
2 WINEGLASSES WHITE WINE
9~10 SAGE LEAVES, CHOPPED

Wash the spinach in several changes of cold water. Cook in a covered saucepan for 15 minutes. Cool, chop and put through a coarse sieve. Melt the butter in a frying pan & gently sauté the spinach for about 10 minutes. Remove from heat & stir in the bechamel, egg yolk, nutmeg, parmesan, salt and pepper. Fold in the egg whites and pour into a deep baking dish, buttered & dusted with breadcrumbs. Place in a bain marie & bake in an oven preheated to 400°F/200°C/ Gas Mark 6 for 20 minutes, or until golden on top.

In the meantime sauté the onion in olive oil over a medium heat. When just golden, turn up the heat & add chicken livers and sage. Cook for a few minutes, until the liver has turned pale. Remove from pan & keep hot. Add the wine and boil briskly until reduced by half, stirring in the bits from the pan. Return the livers to the pan, stir quickly, add salt & pepper & remove from heat. Turn the sformato out onto a dish (it should now have a crunchy golden crust) & pour the livers into the middle. Serve immediately.

· GINESTRATA ·
Chicken and wine cordial (4)

In the spring in Tuscany the perfume of wild broom, ginestra, is overpowering and the roads are lined with huge bushes covered in the brilliant yellow blossoms. These flowers give their name to a famous Tuscan soup that was once endowed with miraculous powers. It could supposedly increase potency, cure disease and improve the powers of the brain (essential after too much Chianti the night before). Although it was & is a recipe particularly associated with the Chianti region where the ginestra blooms most profusely, they make a similar soup at the Buca di San Francesco called 'cordiale'. It lays equal claims to renew vigour & health in just one bowlful.

4 EGGS
2 OZ/50 G BUTTER
1 WINEGLASS OF MARSALA OR VIN SANTO
3/4 PINT/1/2 LITRE GOOD HOME MADE CHICKEN STOCK
1/2 TSP CINNAMON
PINCH OF SAFFRON
PINCH OF NUTMEG
JUICE OF 1/2 LEMON
SUGAR

Beat the eggs and while mixing steadily, slowly add marsala, chicken stock, cinnamon & saffron. Heat gently and add butter cut in small pieces. Continue to mix and when it begins to thicken remove from heat and pour into pretty cups. Stir in lemon juice and sprinkle with sugar and nutmeg.

81

· FOCACCIA ·
Savoury flat bread (4~6)

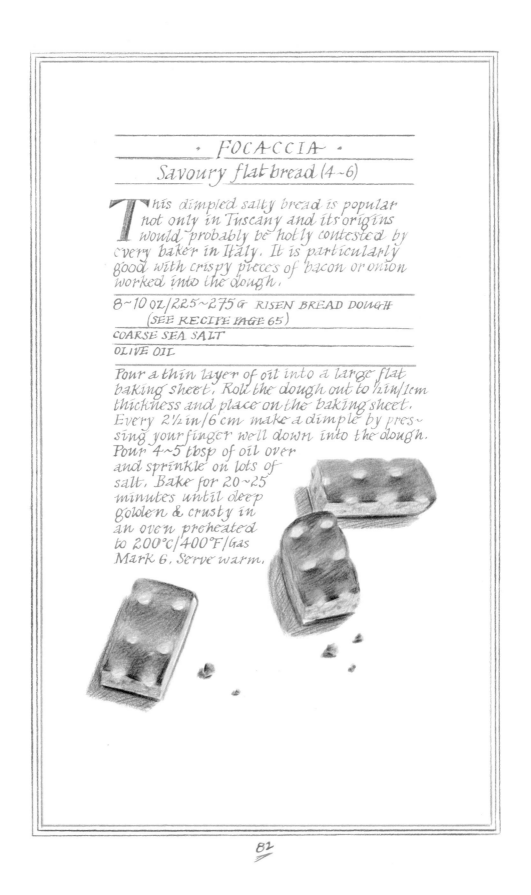

This dimpled salty bread is popular not only in Tuscany and its origins would probably be hotly contested by every baker in Italy. It is particularly good with crispy pieces of bacon or onion worked into the dough.

8~10 OZ/225~275 G RISEN BREAD DOUGH
   (SEE RECIPE PAGE 65)

COARSE SEA SALT

OLIVE OIL

Pour a thin layer of oil into a large flat baking sheet. Roll the dough out to 1/2 in/1 cm thickness and place on the baking sheet. Every 2½ in/6 cm make a dimple by pressing your finger well down into the dough. Pour 4~5 tbsp of oil over and sprinkle on lots of salt. Bake for 20~25 minutes until deep golden & crusty in an oven preheated to 200°C/400°F/Gas Mark 6. Serve warm.

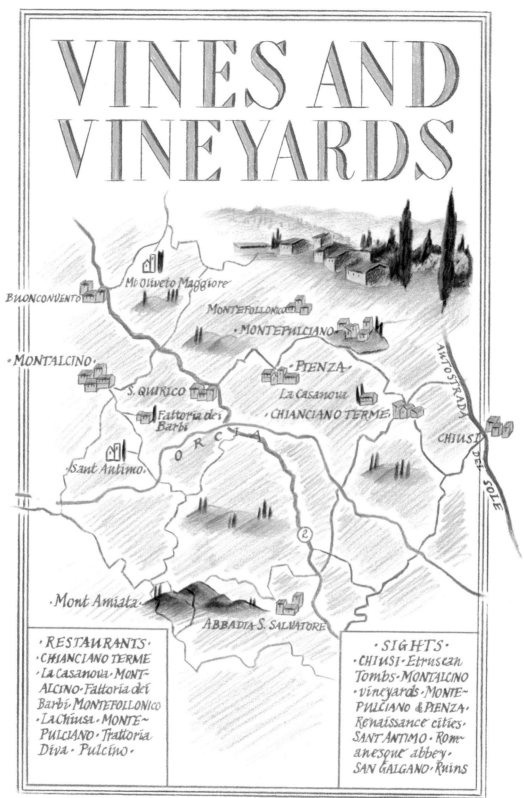

VINES AND VINEYARDS

Mt Oliveto Maggiore

BUONCONVENTO

MONTEFOLLONICO

• MONTEPULCIANO

• MONTALCINO •

S. QUIRICO

• PIENZA •

La Casanova

Fattoria dei Barbi

• CHIANCIANO TERME

AUTOSTRADA

CHIUSI

O R C I A

Sant Antimo •

DEL SOLE

2

• Mont Amiata •

ABBADIA S. SALVATORE

· RESTAURANTS ·
· CHIANCIANO TERME ·
La Casanova · MONT-
ALCINO · Fattoria dei
Barbi · MONTEFOLLONICO
· La Chiusa · MONTE~
PULCIANO · Trattoria
Diva · Pulcino ·

· SIGHTS ·
· CHIUSI · Etruscan
Tombs · MONTALCINO
· vineyards · MONTE~
PULCIANO & PIENZA ·
Renaissance cities ·
SANT ANTIMO · Rom~
anesque abbey ·
SAN GALGANO · Ruins

· INTRODUCTION ·

The area between Montalcino and Montepulciano, south of Siena, is notable not only for the beauty of its countryside and fine Renaissance towns but also for the quality of its wines. Vino Nobile di Montepulciano, an elegant Chianti~style wine, has had its praises sung by poets for centuries. In the seventeenth century the poet~physician Francesco Redi wrote 'Montepulciano d'ogni vino è re'~ Montepulciano of all wines is King. If modern vino nobile is less the king than one of the crown princes of traditional Tuscan wines, it is still worthy of its title. One of the best vino nobiles comes from the little estate of Poderi Boscarelli, lying on the south~eastern slopes of the hill that is crowned by the lovely city of Montepulciano.

Together with its neighbour Pienza, Montepulciano is a model of fifteenth~century town planning. Walk up the main street, the Corso, on a windy spring day and panoramic views of distant vineyards are glimpsed around the corners of impressive baroque palaces. Small balconied piazzas are conveniently designed to open up these views off each of the cobbled streets that climb steeply to the Piazza Grande, the wide and splendid central square that is the highest point in Montepulciano, as well as the focus of the annual music and mime festival every August.

Nine miles to the west of Montepulciano lies Pienza, the ideal city of Piccolomini (Pope Pius II 1458~64), who virtually created the city out of his birthplace, Corsignano. In 1459 he commissioned the Florentine architect Bernardo Rossellino to rebuild the town and make it, and its cathedral, 'the finest in all Italy'. He almost succeeded. Although Piccolomini died before his dream could be realized, he left behind him a beautiful miniature city, complete enough to inspire the director Franco Zeffirelli to use it as the setting for his film of Romeo and Juliet.

Pienza is on the road leading to Montalcino, home of one of the costliest and most prestigious red wines in Italy, Brunello di Montalcino. It has become so in a relatively short time, largely due to the efforts of the Biondi~Santi family. From 1865, when the family first won a citation for a 'Brunello', they have been steadily improving its quality until today it has achieved almost legendary status as a wine whose flavour can outlive some of the longest aged wines in the world. A bottle of Biondi-Santis' Brunello takes years, even decades, to come to full maturity, and if the end result is superb, the cost is prohibitive. Fortunately there are other vineyards producing Brunello at more accessible costs. One of the pleasantest ways to pass a warm autumn afternoon is at Montalcino's elegant little open~air 'Caffe Fiaschetteria Italiana' sampling and discussing vintage Brunellos with the local experts. Or drive through olive and vine~ clad hills of matchless beauty to one of the vineyards open to visitors. The Fattoria dei Barbi is one which has the added advantage of its own excellent trattoria serving local recipes and products from the estate.

The food in the area can vary from Sienese~inspired cuisine at the country restaurant La Chiusa (that also sells olive oil pressed in its own antique 'frantoio' or oil press) to the more robust home~cooking of ribollita and grilled meats at the Fattoria Pulcino near Monte~ pulciano's main gate. There is frequent use of local herbs like tarragon and of the giant porcini mushrooms (BOLETUS EDULIS) picked wild from the slopes of nearby Mont Amiata, an extinct volcano. And the beautiful Ristorante La Casanova near Chian~ ciano Terme has fresh lake fish and imag~ inative game dishes in season.

· TRATTORIA · DIVA ·

PICI DOUGH OF
JUST FLOUR AND
WATER ROLLED WITH
4 FOOT LONG ROLLING
PIN AND THEN DIPPED
IN CORN FLOUR

ADA MAKING
'PICI' ON SATURDAY MORNING
AT DIVA RESTAURANT IN
MONTEPULCIANO WHERE
THE LOCAL FARMERS BRING
ALL THEIR
FRESH
PRODUCE.

SLICED IN
INCH WIDE
STRIPS TO
ROLL WITH
FINGERS
IN YELLOW
CORN
FLOUR

AMAZINGLY LONG
AND WIGGLY LIKE THE
ROADS UP AND DOWN
MONTEPULCIANO.

· MONTEPULCIANO ·

The Trattoria Diva, named after the owner's wife, is a small jolly family~run trattoria near the main gate in Monte~ pulciano. The specialities are simple unpretentious dishes, always accompanied by an excellent selection of local wines from the owner's next door wine enoteca.

· PICI ·
Tuscan eggless pasta (6)

Pici is/are an amazingly time~consuming, completely hand~rolled pasta with no eggs, originally made only by and for the very poor in the area around Montepulciano. They consist of just flour, salt and water. The following is a very approximate recipe.

12 oz / 350 G PLAIN FLOUR, SIFTED
PINCH SALT
SEVERAL TBSP WATER

Knead all the ingredients together to form a stretchy pasta dough. Leave covered for 20 minutes. Roll out until the dough is ¼ in /5mm thick and cut into strips of ½ in/1cm wide. Then work and twist each piece by hand into extremely long and wiggly spaghetti. Keep each string of pasta covered until ready to use. Cook in boiling water in the usual way.

· SALSA di SALSICCIE ·
Sausage sauce (6)

If you can be bothered to make pici, they are an excel- lent and chewy vehicle for this traditional sauce which comes from the foothills of Mont Amiata. And near Chiusi south of Montepulciano pici are eaten tossed in a sauce of 'caviar' from pike caught in the nearby lake.

12 oz/350 G SPICY ITALIAN
  SAUSAGE, SKINNED AND
  CRUMBLED IN PIECES
14 oz / 400 G RIPE TOMATOES,
  PEELED AND MASHED WITH
  A FORK
8 oz/240G FRESH BOLETUS EDULIS
  OR
1oz/25G DRIED 'FUNGHI' MUSHROOMS
  SOAKED IN TEPID WATER 30 MINS
1 LARGE ONION, FINELY CHOPPED
2 TBSP OLIVE OIL
RED WINE (OPTIONAL)

Heat the oil in a shallow flame~proof casserole. Cook the onions in it, and when starting to turn transparent, add the sausages and the mushrooms (squeezed out and sliced if dried). Cook, stirring occasionally, for about ten minutes and then add the tomatoes, salt and pepper to taste and a generous splash of red wine if you like. Cook for another 30 minutes on a low heat. Serve over the cooked, drained pici ~ or any other pasta.

· PICI con CONIGLIO ·
Pasta with rabbit sauce (4)

This, one of the most traditional sauces to serve with pici, can also be used as a sauce with more readily available pastas such as spaghetti or penne.

---

1 OZ / 25 G PANCETTA OR BACON, FINELY CHOPPED
1 LARGE RABBIT, CUT IN PIECES, WITH GIBLETS
1 SMALL ONION, FINELY CHOPPED
1 CARROT, FINELY CHOPPED
2~3 SPRIGS FRESH THYME
1 LB 2 OZ / 500 G TOMATOES, PEELED, SEEDED AND CHOPPED
½ BOTTLE CHIANTI
3 TBSP OLIVE OIL
SALT
PEPPER

Sauté the pancetta, onion and carrot until softened in the oil. Add the rabbit pieces (except the giblets) and brown on all sides. Then add the wine and when nearly evap~ orated the tomatoes and the thyme. Cover and simmer gently until the rabbit is tender ~ about 1~1½ hours. After about half an hour, add the giblets, finely chopped,

and a few tablespoons of warm water or beef stock to ensure that the sauce stays quite liquid. About 10 minutes before the end of cooking remove the rabbit and keep hot. Add the pici and cook through. Or, if using dried pasta, cook the pasta until softened but still firm in boiling water and then add to the sauce. Serve the pasta as a first course with the rabbit to follow, served with spinach and olive oil.

✳ FUNGHI SECCHI ~
(Boletus edulis / Porcini / Ceps)
These huge mushrooms are widely available throughout Tuscany in the late spring & autumn, both in markets & growing wild in woodland clearings (especially on the slopes of Mont Amiata). Their rich flavour is used to enhance everything from peasant stews & simple pasta sauces to elegant veal dishes. Where fresh porcini are not available it is still possible to capture some of their fragrance using dried funghi, 'funghi secchi' (available in packets from many speciality stores).

· FATTORIA · DEI · BARBI ·

In the restaurant of the Fattoria dei Barbi near Montalcino there is an English cook from Bournemouth who makes one of the best bean soups in Tuscany. Even the Tuscans will admit this, which shows how good it must be. It helps that she has been in the country for 20 years, is married to a Tuscan and, even more importantly, has a Tuscan mother~in~law. And it also helps to have the Fattoria products to cook with, herb~flavoured ricotta, fresh pecorino, olive oil, peppery prosciutto, pork steaks for the grill and the famous Barbi/Columbini Brunello wine. It is a good place to go on a hot summer's day, to sit at a check~cloth covered table in the middle of a vineyard and hear the history of Brunello and to follow this with a visit to the beaut~iful old wine cellars, where you may also taste some of the wines.

· ZUPPA di FAGIOLI ·
Tuscan bean soup (6)

This bean soup, a version of the famous 'ribollita' (meaning re~boiled), may well have an even longer history than Brunello wine, & is best made the day be~fore.

- 2 LB 2 OZ /1 KG FRESH CANNELINI (SMALL HARICOT) BEANS OR 14½ OZ/ 420 G DRIED ONES, SOAKED OVERNIGHT
- 3~4 RIPE TOMATOES, PEELED, SEEDED AND MASHED
- 2 STICKS CELERY, FINELY CHOPPED
- 2 CARROTS, FINELY CHOPPED
- 2 LEEKS, FINELY CHOPPED
- 11 OZ /300 G CAVOLO NERO (TUSCAN BLACK CABBAGE) OR YOU CAN SUBSTITUTE SWISS CHARD, SPINACH BEET OR ANY DARK GREEN CABBAGE

(continued)

7 OZ/200 G SAVOY CABBAGE (SAUTED
    SEPARATELY & KEPT FOR TOPPING)
2 CLOVES GARLIC, CRUSHED
2 SPRIGS FRESH THYME
6~8 TBSP OLIVE OIL
STOCK
SALT & PEPPER
6 PIECES HARD STALE BREAD

Boil the beans in plenty of water
until slightly softened. Cover, leave
for an hour & drain. Sieve ¾ into
an equal amount of fresh water &
reserve the rest. Put the oil in a large
saucepan & cook the carrots, celery &
leeks. When soft add the tomatoes,
garlic & thyme. After 5 minutes
add the cabbage, salt & pepper. Cook
about 10 minutes & add the bean
puree & the bean water. Cook slowly
for an hour, adding tepid water if
the soup becomes too solid, although
it should be fairly thick. About 5~
10 minutes before end of cooking,
stir in the whole beans to heat
through & ladle some of the hot
soup over the bread in each bowl.
Serve with cooked cabbage on top,
a bowl of sliced red or spring
onions and a jug of good
green olive oil.

RISOTTO PRIMAVERA
· Spring Risotto (6) ·

This is a very festive looking risotto.

1 LB 2 OZ /500 G ITALIAN ARBORIO RICE
11 OZ/300 G GREENISH TOMATOES,
    DICED
12 OZ/350 G SMALL COURGETTES
    (ZUCCHINI), DICED
7 OZ /200 G GREEN PEPPER OR
    ASPARAGUS, DICED
4 OZ /100 G CARROT, DICED
1 ONION OR LEEK, CHOPPED
BEEF STOCK
5 OZ/150 G BUTTER
2 TBSP OLIVE OIL
SALT & PEPPER

Cook the onion in oil in a sauce~
pan & when beginning to brown,
add all the vegetables except
the tomatoes. Cook 10 minutes
over moderate heat & add tomatoes,
salt & pepper. Cook for 15 minutes &
then pour in the rice & a little hot
stock. Continue adding tablespoons
of hot stock every few minutes as
the rice absorbs the liquid. It
should take 20~30 minutes for the
rice to cook to the
'al dente' stage.
Then stir in
butter &
serve.

Tuscany is justifiably famous for the quality of its meat & fresh vegetable dishes, but less well~known (outside Italy) for the variety of ways in which wild herbs are used for any~thing from pasta filling to souffles or sformati, a Tuscan cross between a souffle and a vegetable mold. These two rec~ipes come from an old lady encountered picking a basket of nettles near Montepulciano.

SFORMATO di ORTICA
· Souffle of Nettles ·
— or spinach (4) —

2 LB 2 OZ / 1 KG TENDER SPRING
    NETTLE LEAVES (OR SPINACH)
4 EGGS, BEATEN
4 OZ / 100 G PARMESAN CHEESE,
    GRATED
PINCH GRATED NUTMEG
4 OZ / 100 G BUTTER
CLOVE GARLIC, CRUSHED
SALT
PEPPER

Wash the nettles under running water for at least half an hour. Boil (save water for soup) for 10~15 minutes until tender, drain well and chop. Melt the butter in a medium~sized pan and saute the nettles, garlic and salt for 5 minutes. Add pepper and nutmeg and put through a food processor or vegetable mill. Stir in the eggs and cheese and pour into a buttered souffle dish. Place in a bain marie or roasting tin with water about ½ in/1cm deep and bake in an oven pre~ heated to 400°F/200°C/Gas 6 for about 30 minutes or until it has risen and is golden brown. Serve immediately.

MINESTRA di PISCIALETTO
· Tuscan Dandelion ·
— greens soup (4) —

Translated literally, piscialetto means pissbed, a Tuscan ref~ erence to the colour of the dandelion flowers and its proximity to passing dogs. Elsewhere, however, it is trad~ itionally regarded as having medicinal properties for humans.

9 OZ / 250 G TINY DANDELION
    LEAVES
2 CLOVES GARLIC, CRUSHED
1 3/4 PT / 1 LTR WATER OR STOCK
LEEK, FINELY CHOPPED
STICK CELERY, FINELY CHOPPED
OLIVE OIL
SALT
BLACK PEPPER

Saute the onion, garlic and celery in oil in a medium~ sized pan. When softened, add the dandelion leaves (keep a few for garnishing the soup), washed well and chopped. Cook for 5 minutes and then add water or stock, salt and pepper, cook for half an hour and then put through a food processor or vegetable mill. It can then be re~ heated and served over toasted bread.

BORAGINE

SANT ANTIMO
· Wild Herbs ·

One of the loveliest & most
peaceful sights in Tuscany
is the Benedictine abbey of
Sant Antimo. Set in a golden
green valley south of Montalcino,
this French~Romanesque church
was founded, according to tradition,
by Charlemagne sometime in the
ninth century. Legend has it
that at the same time
Charlemagne also introduced
tarragon or 'dragoncello' as
a cooking herb in the region
between Montalcino and
Siena. Tarragon, essentially
a French herb, is rarely used
anywhere else in Tuscany but
is found growing abundantly
near Sant Antimo, as is the

more common wild borage. The
young tender leaves and vivid
blue flowers of borage can
be cooked as fritters
(like the zucchini
flower fritters on
page 70), tossed in
salads with other wild
greens such as dandelions
or sautéed gently in oil
and added to beaten
eggs to make a borage
frittata. Tuscan frittatas,
although similar in some
ways to French omelettes,
differ in that they are
cooked slowly until firm
over a low heat and are
then usually grilled
quickly to set the top
side. They are often
served as a light
evening meal with a
selection of antipasti,
but also make an
interesting alternative to
sandwiches when served
cold on a picnic.

DRAGONCELLO

95

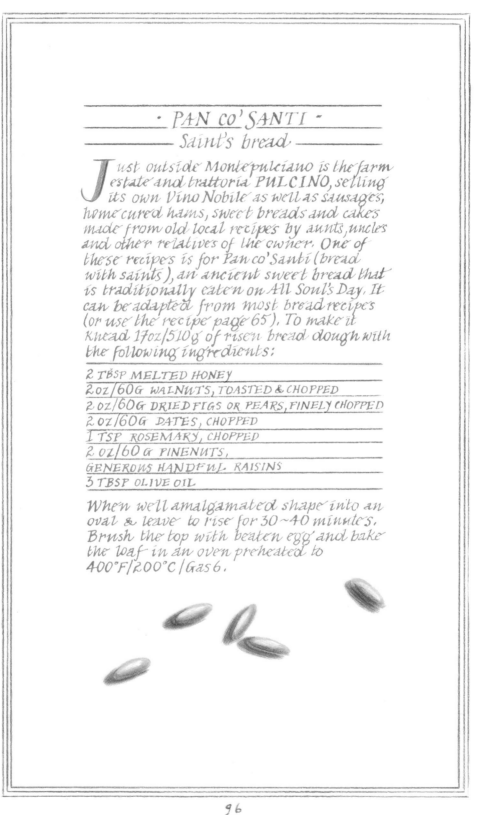

· PAN CO' SANTI ·
— Saint's bread —

Just outside Montepulciano is the farm estate and trattoria PULCINO, selling its own Vino Nobile as well as sausages, home cured hams, sweet breads and cakes made from old local recipes by aunts, uncles and other relatives of the owner. One of these recipes is for Pan co' Santi (bread with saints), an ancient sweet bread that is traditionally eaten on All Soul's Day. It can be adapted from most bread recipes (or use the recipe page 65). To make it knead 17oz/510g of risen bread dough with the following ingredients:

2 TBSP MELTED HONEY	
2 OZ/60G WALNUTS, TOASTED & CHOPPED	
2 OZ/60G DRIED FIGS OR PEARS, FINELY CHOPPED	
2 OZ/60G DATES, CHOPPED	
1 TSP ROSEMARY, CHOPPED	
2 OZ/60 G PINENUTS,	
GENEROUS HANDFUL RAISINS	
3 TBSP OLIVE OIL	

When well amalgamated shape into an oval & leave to rise for 30~40 minutes. Brush the top with beaten egg and bake the loaf in an oven preheated to 400°F/200°C/Gas 6.

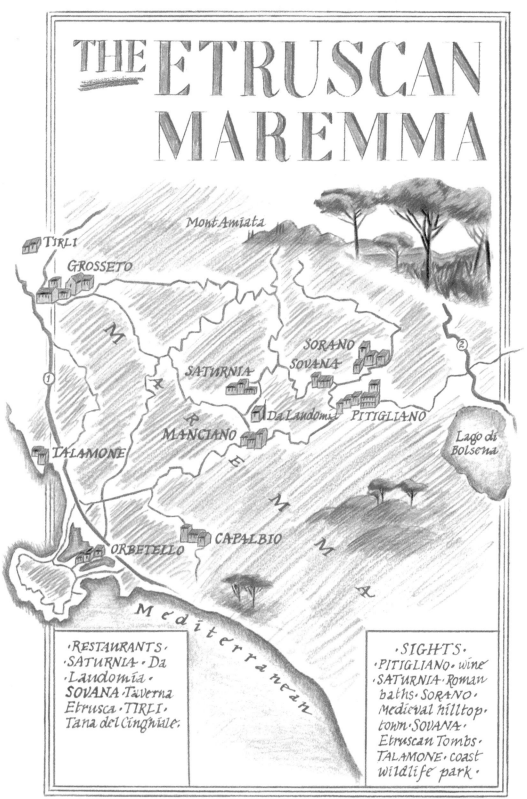

THE ETRUSCAN MAREMMA

Mont Amiata

TIRLI

GROSSETO

SORANO

SOVANA

SATURNIA

Da Laudomia   PITIGLIANO

MANCIANO

Lago di Bolsena

TALAMONE

CAPALBIO

ORBETELLO

Mediterranean

·RESTAURANTS·
·SATURNIA· Da
·Laudomia·
SOVANA ·Taverna
Etrusca ·TIRLI·
Tana del Cinghiale·

·SIGHTS·
·PITIGLIANO· wine
·SATURNIA· Roman
baths· SORANO·
Medieval hilltop·
town ·SOVANA·
Etruscan Tombs·
TALAMONE· coast
wildlife park·

· INTRODUCTION ·

Driving through the wide meadows and gently rolling low hills that are the Tuscan Maremma today, it is almost impossible to believe that less than a hundred years ago much of this now fertile countryside was malaria~ridden marshland. During Etruscan times the area northeast of the principal city of Grosseto was a navigable gulf. By the middle ages this had become a freshwater lake, which in turn became a swamp, causing widespread disease and famine. Many unsuccessful efforts were made to reclaim the land but it was not until the early years of this century that the Maremma was effectively rid of the malaria that had wiped out whole towns. In the 1950s a systematic government programme of agricultural incentives and repopulation was begun and the area's past prosperity virtually restored. Today the Etruscan-red soil produces abundant flowers, vegetables, grains and grapes.

The word 'Maremma' means coastal plain and, apart from the modern resorts along the coast, the area was probably more densely populated in Etruscan times, 2000 years ago, than it is now. Certainly evidence of these earliest settlers of Tuscany is everywhere. They left behind their name for the country, 'Tuscia', as well as many of their tombs and burial sites. At the lonely semi~abandoned village of Sovana the single-story medieval houses seem less inhabited than the Etruscan necropolis set in a cool birch gulley a mile away. Five miles to the south~east, Sovana's gloomy & forbidding neighbour, Pitigliano, grows out of a magnificent rocky mountain~top whose base is riddled with caves that were once Etruscan and Roman tombs but now serve as cellars for the excellent Pitigliano white wine. The three deep ravines around the town formed a natural moat when this town was the seat of the Roman Orsini barons during the thirteenth century.

The Etruscans were not the only settlers to leave their mark on the land. During the mid~1500s, when Orbetello was the capital of the Spanish Garrison States, pirates from the Barbary coast were a constant hazard along the coast and close to the sea are the crumbling remains of a few towers from which watch was kept for the invaders. Despite these precautions however, one night in April 1543, the beautiful young daughter of a local family, the Marsilis, was kidnapped by Barbarossa's pirates and survived to become the favourite wife of Sultan Solimani. And at Orbetello many of the present~day inhabitants still retain the swarthy good looks of Moorish forbears.

Much of the Maremman coast has been ruined by expensive resort developments but fortunately some of the original terrain is protected by the Monti dell' Uccellina, the Maremman Nature Reserve. In this long stretch of wood & scrubland wildlife flourishes and the huge umbrella pines, so typical of the area, shade miles of white deserted beaches. It is possible to see hare, deer and porcupines, and most unexpectedly, herds of long~horn cattle & wild horses rounded up by 'butteri', the cowboys of the Maremma. At the medieval town of Capalbio these cowboys have their own riders fair in October.

Capalbio is the main centre of horsebreeding in southern Tuscany and also an excellent place to sample wild game prepared in appetizing local recipes. But throughout the Maremma game is readily available. During the autumn hunting season small family restaurants, Da Laudomia near Saturnia and the Taverna Etrusca in Sovana, serve hearty toe~warming dishes that make use not only of the plentiful wild boar and roebuck but also of fresh local herbs, tomatoes and wild mushrooms. Garlic is used here far more than in the rest of Tuscany, perhaps because it is a cheap way of adding flavour to a simple dish. The Maremman people do not easily forget that their region has only very recently become agriculturally rich after centuries of much hardship.

For centuries the Tuscans, some of the world's most avid hunters, shot anything that moved: wild boar, deer, pheasant, thrushes, porcupines and even hedgehogs. And then it usually reappeared on the table. Now there is an increasing reluctance to wipe out songbirds. There is much less reluctance, however, to halt the hunting of wild boar, or cinghiale, which, being large and quite fierce, provides more sport than a songbird. All over Tuscany you can buy delicious hams and sausages made from this tasty meat, particularly in the Maremma where the broom~covered hills provide excellent cinghiale cover. The recipes below come from the cook at the Tana del Cinghiale, a remote hunting lodge at the tiny village of Tirli in the Maremman hills.

CINGHIALE alle MELE
Wild boar with apples (6)

Wild boar, unless very young and tender, needs to be marin~ated, but before that it should have been hung for a few days. Ask your butcher or game dealer, he should know its history.

2½ LB/1·2 KG WILD BOAR ~ THE RIB MEAT FOR PREFERENCE
3~4 LARGE COOKING APPLES, PEELED, CORED & SLICED
1 ONION, CHOPPED
2 GLASSES RED WINE
SMALL PIECE CHILI PEPPER
CARROT, CHOPPED
CELERY STICK, CHOPPED
SALT
FRESH ROSEMARY
FRESH THYME
OLIVE OIL
ABOUT 1¾ PT/ 1 LTR BEEF STOCK

· MARINADE ·

1 ¾ PT/1 LTR RED WINE
¼ PT/150 ML VINEGAR
3¼ PT/1.75 LTR WATER
5~6 BAY LEAVES
½ TSP CINNAMON
6 WHOLE PEPPERCORNS
4 LEAVES FRESH MINT
2 OZ/50 G SEA SALT
3~4 SPRIGS FRESH ROSEMARY
3~4 SPRIGS FRESH THYME

Combine all the ingredients for the marinade. Cut the meat into chunks and completely cover in the marinade. Add more wine if the meat is not covered. Leave for three days in a refrigerator and stir often. If it begins to give an unpleas~ant smell, change the liquid~this is not a 'cucina povera' dish. After three days rinse well in warm water. Heat the oil in a heat~proof casserole and add the onion, carrot, celery, chili and herbs. When soft add the meat, salt and pepper, and brown well. Pour in the red wine and when slightly evaporated lower the heat and add a cup of beef stock. Cover and cook gently for 2~3 hours, until tender, adding stock as necessary to prevent it drying out. Half an hour before the end of cooking, pack the apples over the meat. Recover and finish cooking. Serve over toasted bread or deep fried polenta (see page 49).

LEPRE in DOLCE e FORTE
· Hare in strong · sweet sauce (6)

This classic way of cooking both boar and hare requires a strong wild meat. The quan~tities are for the more readily available hare. The dish has a strange, exotic taste and is much better made the day before it is required. Be sure of your guest's capabilities before serving it ~ it is definitely not nouvelle cuisine.

1 LARGE HARE, CLEANED
2 OZ/50 G PANCETTA, FINELY
  CHOPPED
3 SPRIGS THYME
GOOD BEEF OR CHICKEN STOCK
OLIVE OIL
11 OZ/300 G TOMATOES
2 TBSP CHOPPED PARSLEY
LARGE WINEGLASS WHITE WINE
2 CRUMBLED BAY LEAVES

· MARINADE ·

1 PT/½ LTR WHITE WINE
WINEGLASS OF WHITE
  WINE VINEGAR
ONION STUCK WITH 4 CLOVES
CELERY STICK, SLICED
CARROT, SLICED
CLOVE GARLIC, CRUSHED
3 JUNIPER BERRIES
6 PEPPERCORNS
(continued...)

PECORINO MAREMMANO
£ 12.00 L'ETTO

0.66 CINGHIALE

SALSA AGRODOLCE

2 TBSP GRANULATED SUGAR

2 TBSP WATER

2 TBSP RED WINE VINEGAR

2 OZ/50 G BITTER COOKING
    CHOCOLATE

1½ OZ/40 G RAISINS, SOAKED

2½ OZ/60 G PINENUTS

2 TBSP MIXED CANDIED LEMON
    AND ORANGE PEEL

Combine all the ingredients for the marinade. Cut the hare in pieces, wash well and cover with the marinade for 24 hours, stirring often. Drain, wash and dry the hare. Heat a little oil in a flame proof casserole, add the thyme, parsley, bay leaves & finely chopped pancetta & soften. Then add the hare & saute well. Add salt, pour in a glass of wine & when it has evaporated add the tomatoes. Cover & cook slowly over a low heat for at least 2 hours, adding hot stock as needed to stop the stew drying out. About half an hour before the hare has finished cooking, melt the sugar with water over low heat until slightly brown. Add the chocolate melted in the vinegar, and after a few minutes the raisins, pinenuts & peel. Mix well & take from the heat. Remove hare from the liquid, & sieve or liquidize the remaining juices. Return meat & sauce to the casserole & slowly add the agrodolce. Heat through for 10 minutes & serve with a crisp borage salad.

CIPOLLE alla GROSSETANA
· Stuffed onions ·
Grosseto style (4)

This recipe has hundreds of variations in the Maremma. Some cooks substitute half a finely chopped chili pepper for the nutmeg & cinnamon, some add ½ oz/15 g dried mushrooms, soaked, squeezed out & chopped. Whatever variation you use, these onions make a good lunch for a cold winter's day.

4 LARGE OR 8 SMALL WHITE ONIONS

4 OZ/125 G LEAN BEEF, GROUND
    OR MINCED

BUTTER

OLIVE OIL

SALT & PEPPER

¼ TSP NUTMEG

4 OZ/125 G GROUND SPICY SAUSAGE

1 EGG

1 WINE GLASS DRY WHITE WINE

4 TBSP GRATED PECORINO OR
    PARMESAN CHEESE *

¼ TSP CINNAMON

Peel the onions and boil until slightly softened in salted water (about 10 minutes). Trim enough off one end so the onions will stand upright. Remove a little of the other end & most of the inside, leaving just a shell. Chop the remaining onion finely & saute in butter with the beef and sausage until brown. Stir in the spices and wine. When the wine has nearly evaporated, turn off the heat and leave to cool. Then mix the sauce with egg and cheese and stuff the onion shells with this. Bake at a moderate heat, 350°F/180°C/Gas 4, in an oiled baking dish for about 25 minutes until brown, moistening with water or stock if the onions seem to be burning.

* It is also good to serve this dish with several tablespoons of bechamel sauce instead of cheese.

102

103

DA LAUDOMIA

One hundred years ago Da Laudomia was a small posting inn (called Locanda Butelli after the present owner's grand~parents) where tired travellers stopped to eat, change horses and buy anything from trousers to home~made sweets. The store and the horses have gone, but Da Laudomia remains much the same (des~pite the change of name) and the present patronne, Clara Detti, can tell you more about the history & the

practice of Maremman cooking than can be found
in any book on the subject.

· ACQUACOTTA ·

Tomato and bread soup (4)

Signora Detti believes that Acquacotta (literally 'cooked water')
began when itinerant carbonari
or charcoal-burners worked
through the winters in the
Maremma. They were so poor
that they lived in igloos of twigs
built around their ever-burning
charcoal fires, and over each of
these fires hung a pot of
simmering water. Any food
that could be scrounged or
exchanged for charcoal was put
in this pot ~ usually garlic,
stale bread and onions, but as
times got better, tomatoes,
celery and an egg or two went
in. From these humble
beginnings Acquacotta has
evolved into this slightly
more sophisticated version
without losing its original
simplicity. There are an
almost infinite number of
variations to this soup, one
of the best is the addition
of several dried
mushrooms
and one
spicy
grilled
sausage per
person at the
beginning of
(continued...)

105

(continued from previous page) cooking. But whatever variation you follow, this soup always tastes best if eaten when you are tired and hungry.

2~3 LARGE ONIONS, FINELY CHOPPED
1 LB 10 OZ / 750 G TOMATOES, PEELED
    AND DESEEDED (OR A MIXTURE
    OF 11 OZ / 300 G SWEET RED PEPPERS
    AND 1 LB / 450 G TOMATOES)
5~6 STICKS CELERY, DICED
    (INCLUDING THE LEAVES)
4 TBSP GOOD OLIVE OIL
1 3/4 PT / 1 LTR BOILING SALTED WATER
4 EGGS
8 PIECES STALE BREAD, TOASTED (OR
    FRIED IN OLIVE OIL IF YOU ARE
    NOT TOO WEIGHT CONSCIOUS)
SALT & PEPPER

Heat the olive oil in a medium saucepan and cook the onion & celery over a low heat until just beginning to brown. Add the tomatoes, salt and pepper and cook for 20 minutes. Pour in the boiling water and leave to simmer. Meanwhile toast (or fry) the bread and put on the bottom of a fireproof soup tureen. When the soup tastes good (after about 30 minutes) put the tureen over a low heat and pour the soup over the bread. Then break each egg separately into the soup, spacing them well apart and taking care that the yolks do not break. (For safety's sake you can break the eggs into a cup first.) Serve the soup as soon as the eggs have set, with plenty of freshly grated parmesan or pecorino cheese sprinkled over.

· MAIALE con LATTE ·
Pork with milk (4)

As this dish is served at Da Laudomia, the sauce at the end has a slightly curdled appearance. If this offends you, sieve the cooked sauce and reheat gently before serving it.

---

2 LB 2 OZ / 1 KG LOIN OF PORK, BONED
4 OZ / 100 KG BUTTER
1 LARGE TOMATO, PEELED, SEEDED
    AND FINELY CHOPPED
3 LEEKS, FINELY CHOPPED
1 STICK CELERY, DICED WITH LEAVES
2 LARGE SPRIGS FRESH THYME
1 3/4 PT / 1 LTR MILK
SALT & PEPPER
FLOUR
CLOVE GARLIC, CRUSHED

Melt the butter in a casserole large enough to hold all the ingredients. Put in the celery, leeks, garlic and tomatoes. Cook over a low heat until the celery and leeks have softened. Meanwhile snip the thyme over the pork, roll the meat up with the thyme inside, tie it with string and rub salt & pepper well into the skin. Roll tightly in the flour and brown over a low heat in the casserole with the vegetables. While it is browning, heat the milk almost to boiling and pour over the meat. Cover & cook for about 2 hours, or until the meat is tender, in an oven preheated to 350°F/180°C/Mark 4. Check occasionally to see the milk does not burn. If the meat seems to be drying out, add a few tbsps of water. To serve, slice the meat thickly & pour the sauce over it, after scraping all the meat from the casserole & stirring it in.

At Mario and Nadia Lupi's bar on the cliffs of Sorano, they make Gli Sfratti, a honey~filled sweet, at Christmas.

· GLI SFRATTI ·

Sweet walnut rolls (2 dozen)

This delicious sweet is extremely ancient in origin. As far as it can be traced, the Etruscans enjoyed it as much as the 'Gioca' playing customers in the Lupis' bar.

FOR THE PASTRY
4 OZ/110 G GRANULATED SUGAR
4 OZ/110 G COLD BUTTER, CUT IN
    SMALL PIECES
9 OZ/250 G PLAIN FLOUR
1 EGG, BEATEN
PINCH OF BICARBONATE OF SODA
2 TBSP MILK (APPROXIMATE)
GRATED PEEL OF ½ LEMON

FOR THE FILLING
9 OZ/250 G HONEY
9 OZ/250 G WALNUTS, CHOPPED
    VERY FINELY
1 OZ/25 G FINE BREADCRUMBS
GRATED PEEL OF ½ LEMON

First make the stuffing. Cook the honey over a low heat for 20 minutes. Add the walnuts and continue cooking for a further 10 minutes. Stir in the bread~crumbs and lemon peel very thoroughly and put the mixture in the refrigerator to cool. Meanwhile make the pastry. Sift the flour and bicarbonate together together onto a pastryboard or worksurface. Mix in the sugar, make a well in the middle & into this put the egg, lemon peel and butter. Rub this in and knead it to form a stiff dough, adding a little milk if necessary to keep it pliable. Put aside and chill for about 30 minutes. Then roll the dough out very thinly and trim to a width of 2 in/5 cm. Spread with a thin layer of the filling mixture. Roll the dough up carefully to form a long finger. Trim to fit onto a greased baking sheet and brush all over with beaten egg yolk. Bake in an oven preheated to 400°F/200°C/Gas 6 for 15 minutes until golden. Cool on a wire rack and serve sliced into 'fingers' or rounds.

107

TORTINO di POMODORI
Hot tomato pie (4)

This simple recipe from Tuscany's south bears a strong resemblance to the Basque dish 'piperade' without the ham. It is best cooked in the dish it will be served in and then carried, still sizzling, straight to the table.

6 EGGS, BEATEN
4 RIPE TOMATOES, PEELED, SEEDED
   AND CHOPPED
1/4 ~ 1/2 HOT CHILI PEPPER,
   FINELY CHOPPED
1 CLOVE GARLIC, CRUSHED
4~5 FRESH BASIL LEAVES, TORN
   IN SMALL PIECES
1/2 ONION, FINELY CHOPPED
OLIVE OIL
SALT & PEPPER
GRATED PECORINO CHEESE

Cook the onion, garlic and chili pepper in oil over a low heat. When softened but not brown add the tomatoes and the basil. Cover and leave to cook just until the tomatoes look slightly mashed. Add beaten eggs, salt and pepper to taste and leave to set. When it is firm throughout but still creamy on top, sprinkle on several tablespoons of cheese and put under a hot grill until bubbling. Serve it piping hot with more basil on top and plenty of fresh crusty bread.

✳ Another simple & good 'tortino' is made by mixing 2 1/2 tbsp flour, 7 tbsp milk, 5 tsp granulated sugar & 2 sliced apples. Fry in butter like an omelette & dust with sugar.

...My dear abbot, twixt cakes and soups
so much cheese have you my body imbued
that should I continue my stay with you
I would Paulo cease to be and a form
    of cheese would I assume.
(ATTRIBUTED TO PAULO UCCELLO WHEN HE WAS WORKING ON A
FRESCO FOR THE ABBOT OF SAN MINIATO)

It seems likely that Uccello's surfeit was of pecorino, the pungent cheese made of sheeps milk whose origins date back to Roman times. It is still the most popular and widely available cheese in Tuscany. Some people would say too popular. There are over 100 different varieties but when trying them be open-minded. Creamy yellow Maremman pecorino is excellent & may seem more appetizing, but equally good are the small Siena cheeses with hard red rinds, & the mold covered pecorino that has absorbed different flavours from the leaves in which it has been wrapped to mature. All pecorino cheeses change character with age, varying from a Gouda-like consistency when young or 'fresco' to a pungent crumbly Parmesan texture when mature.

OLIO all'ARRABIATA
'Enraged' oil •

If you are unsure of your own or your friends' liking for hot chili pepper, fill a small stoppered bottle 3/4 full of olive oil and into it put a couple of whole chili peppers (slightly bruised). Left for several days, the chili will 'enrage' the oil enough to satisfy any hot~ blooded person. Serve as a condiment at the table so every~ one can add a few drops, or not to their own taste. This is a particularly good idea when serving Fettunta (page 29) or any of the robust Tuscan soups like Pappa al Pomodoro.

BY THE SEA

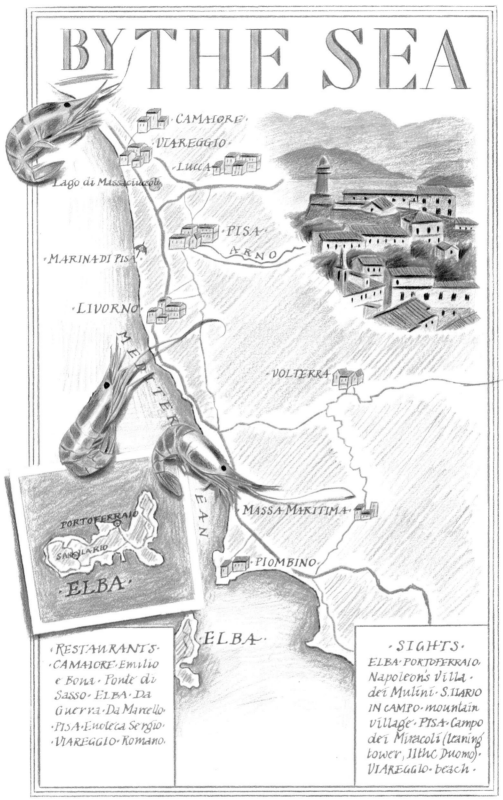

· CAMAIORE ·
· VIAREGGIO ·
· LUCCA ·
Lago di Massaciucoli

· MARINA DI PISA ·

· LIVORNO ·

PISA
ARNO

MEDITER

VOLTERRA

PORTOFERRAIO

SAN ILARIO

· ELBA ·

MASSA MARITIMA

ELBA

· PIOMBINO ·

· RESTAURANTS ·
· CAMAIORE · Emilio
e Bona · Ponte di
Sasso · ELBA · Da
Guerra · Da Marcello
· PISA · Enoteca Sergio
· VIAREGGIO · Romano ·

· SIGHTS ·
ELBA · PORTOFERRAIO ·
Napoleon's Villa ·
dei Mulini · S. ILARIO
IN CAMPO · mountain
village · PISA · Campo
dei Miracoli (leaning
tower, 11thc Duomo) ·
VIAREGGIO · beach ·

· INTRODUCTION ·

An hour by ferry from the Tuscan Maremma lies mountainous Elba, the largest island in the Tuscan archipelago. Its huge supply of iron ore provides much of Italy's requirement and has been mined on the island for at least 3000 years. The main port was called Portoferraio (Port Iron) as early as the eigth century and the rich palette of Elba's wines is due to the high iron content in the soil.

Possibly because of this mineral wealth, Elba has been in turn invaded & settled by the Sicilians, Etruscans, Romans, Moors, Spanish, Pisans & finally, of course, by the French under Napoleon. It is not surprising then that the island's cuisine is such a melting pot of cookery styles, each with its own distinctive Elban twist. It is possible to eat 'puttenaio', a ratatouille-like vegetable stew, in Portoferraio, or 'la sburrida', a fish soup of Spanish origin in Capoliveri, where legend has it that Cosimo de' Medici promised sixteenth-century Spanish pirates he would leave their favourite haunt unharassed if they would do the same for his town of Cosmopolia.

Not all past visitors to Elba were military ones. The tourist trade certainly existed in 1914. In a book, Napoleon's Elba, published in that year, an English-woman, Lydia Bushnell Smith, mentions buying '...the obligatory picture card of the island.' But it was not until later in this century that tourists began coming to Elba for its fine sandy beaches instead of its Napoleonic associations.

Livorno, the major Tuscan commercial port, is less likely to suffer change than Elba as a result of the tourist trade. The 'ideal city' created by the Medici grand dukes suffered heavy bombing during World War 2, losing in the process much of its charm along with many of its fine buildings. The sixteenth-century foreigners who knew and loved Livorno under the old English name 'Leghorn' would barely recognize it today. Still one of the greatest ports in the Mediterranean, it is now best known for its famous fish dishes 'alla Livornese', rich with tomatoes, parsley and garlic, a style of cooking whose influence can be appreciated along most of the Tuscan coast.

On the river Arno, a few miles north, lies Pisa, a thriving port when Livorno was still a small medieval fishing village. Thriving, that is, until 1284, when Pisa's navy was destroyed in battle, & its government allowed the harbour to fill with silt. Now Pisa lies miles inland, no longer a port but a university town, one of the most respected in Italy. The university's science faculty is as strong today as it was when Galileo dropped 3 metal balls from the top of the famous leaning bell tower, the Campanile, to disprove Aristotle's theories about the acceleration of falling objects. The Campanile, along with the black & white pyjama-striped Duomo, the lovely Baptistry & the vast cemetery is both the tourist & the ecclesiastical centre of the city. But the heart of Pisa must be the market area sprawling over a maze of streets north of the Arno. Here medieval buildings lean crazily over the pavements to form narrow tunnels linking piazzas. Foreign university students jostle stout Pisan housewives for freshest mullet & tiniest 'Cee', the local name for the tiny eels that are a speciality.

The poet Percy Bysse Shelley lived for years in Tuscany & wrote some of his best poems in Pisa in the 1800s. He described the region as a 'paradise of exiles', a particularly apt description of the coastal resort Viareggio. During the summer the city's famous square, the Piazza Shelley, fills with parties of English tourists, standing mournfully in front of the poet's monument. It records that in 1822 Shelley's drowned body was washed up on Viareggio's beach, a fact that doesn't deter these same mournful tourists from later dining well in one of Viareggio's excellent fish restaurants.

When the defeated Nap~oleon arrived on Elba, he immediately set about turning his island prison into a setting more suitable for an emperor~ even if a deposed one. One of the first things he did was to convert two old windmills into the lovely villa 'Palazzino dei Mulini', which still stands today, surrounded by palm trees and cypresses on top of the hill at Portoferraio.

· PUTTENAIO ·
Prostitutes' stew (4)

Napoleon's stay, short though it was, brought a decidedly French influence to the island's cooking. Evidence is this vegetable stew, derogatorily called 'Puttenaio' (prostitute's stew) which bears a distinct resemblance to the famous French ratatouille.

1 LB 6 OZ / 600 G GREEN PEPPERS
2 LARGE POTATOES
2 AUBERGINES (EGGPLANTS)
1 STICK CELERY
CARROT
LARGE ONION
1 LB 6 OZ / 600 G RIPE TOMATOES, PEELED AND SEEDED
2 ZUCCHINI (COURGETTES)
1/4 PT OLIVE OIL
SMALL HANDFUL OF FRESH HERBS SUCH AS PARSLEY, ROSEMARY, THYME OR BASIL
COARSE SEA SALT
2 CLOVES GARLIC, CRUSHED

Cut the onion into thin slices and the rest of the vegetables into rough chunks. Heat the oil in a large saucepan and cook everything except the tomatoes and the herbs for 10~15 minutes. Add the salt and tomatoes, cover and cook over a high heat for 10 minutes. Then simmer for about 1 hour. 15 minutes before the end of cooking add the fresh herbs. This is an excellent dish served hot or cold with boiled meat.

∗ If the tomatoes are not very tasty it is a good idea to add several tablespoons of a good tomato purée at the start of cooking.

· PESCI ARROSTO ·
Grilled fish (4)

There is a story that Napoleon, on one of his frequent restless walks around Porto~ferraio, stopped to admire a catch brought in by some fishermen. The emperor was known to like simple people and simple food. After a chat with the men he invited them back to dinner at the Villa Mulini. And the dinner that night was their own fish! This recipe for grilled fresh sardines comes from Signora Pierangela Piras' excellent book L'ISOLA D'ELBA IN CUCINA, but it is such a

(continued ...)

(continued from previous page...) classic way of cooking fish that it could well have been served that night.

FRESH SARDINES, THE NUMBER PER PERSON DEPENDING ON WHETHER THEY ARE BEING SERVED AS A STARTER OR A MAIN DISH
TSP SEA SALT
CLOVE GARLIC
3 TBSP OLIVE OIL
4 OZ/100 G FENNEL BULB & LEAVES, FINELY CHOPPED
1/2 HOT CHILI PEPPER
1 TBSP WHITE WINE VINEGAR

Clean, scale and thoroughly wash the fish, Make a marinade by crushing all the remaining ingredients together in a mortar, adding more oil if necessary. Put fish in the marinade and leave it for 30~40 minutes, turning often. Grill the fish, turning once only and basting frequently with the marinade oil. If using a grilling rack, wipe it with oil first so the fish don't stick.

Quite understandably, these fish taste best cooked over a wood fire (the Tuscans use chestnut which is particularly aromatic) but if you must use charcoal, try throwing fresh herbs on it to scent both the air & the fish.

S. ILARIO. IN. CAMPO

· ZUCCHINI RIPIENO ·
Stuffed zucchini/courgettes (4)

This delicious Elban method of cooking the first young spring zucchini is equally good using small aubergines (eggplants) instead. Or serve a big mixed plateful with whole zucchini flower fritters.

8 TINY ZUCCHINI
7 OZ/200 G GROUND LEAN BEEF
4 OZ/100 G CHOPPED MORTADELLA
OLIVE OIL
OIL FOR DEEP FRYING
4 EGGS, BEATEN
4 TBSP GRATED PARMESAN
2 TBSP FRESH THYME, CHOPPED
2 CLOVES GARLIC, CRUSHED
1½ CUPS (APPROX) FINE BREAD
   CRUMBS

Boil the whole zucchini for 2~3 minutes until just tender. Cut in half lengthwise and remove the pulp. In a frying pan heat the olive oil and cook the beef and garlic until browned and then mix with mortadella, zucchini pulp, cheese, thyme and 2 eggs. Stuff the zucchini with this mixture and tie the two halves together with thread. Dip each stuffed zucchini into beaten egg and then roll in breadcrumbs until well covered. Deep fry or bake in a hot oven preheated to 450°F/230°C/Gas 8 until crisp and brown. Remove the thread before eating.

People come from all over Elba to eat at Marcello's small and cosy fish restaurant on the waterfront in the fishing village of Marciana Marina. There he serves fresh fish and regional specialities to both regular customers and discerning visitors.

SPAGHETTI alla MARINARA
Spaghetti & seafood sauce (4)

This is a loose interpretation of Marcello's delicious recipe, but it can be varied according to the season and individual taste, including crab and lobster, although that seems rather an extravagance.

1 LB/450 G THINNEST SPAGHETTI
4 OZ/100 G OCTOPUS
4 OZ/100 G CUTTLEFISH WITHOUT THE INKSAC
1 LB 2 OZ/500 G MUSSELS
1 LB 2 OZ/500 G ARSELLE (BABY CLAMS), SOAKED OVERNIGHT IN SALT WATER
3 TBSP FRESH CHOPPED PARSLEY
2 CLOVES GARLIC, CRUSHED
1~2 GLASSES DRY WHITE WINE
6 TBSP OLIVE OIL
SALT
1 ONION, FINELY CHOPPED

Cook half the mussels in a little water until just beginning to open. Keep half the mussels and all the clams aside. Clean the cuttlefish and octopus and chop finely. Remove the cooked mussels from their shells and chop finely. Heat the oil in a medium-sized pan and saute the onion. When soft add the octopus, cuttlefish and chopped mussels. Cook for about 5 minutes and then add the wine. When partially evaporated, put in the garlic and parsley. After 10 minutes add the clams and mussels in their shells, adjust salt and cook for another 5~10 minutes or until they have all opened. Discard any that remain closed. Meanwhile put the spaghetti on to cook in boiling salted water. When just cooked, drain and toss with the sauce. Serve with more chopped parsley sprinkled on top.

· DA GUERRA ·

The Elbans claim it never rains in summer. Don't believe them, it can and it does. But if you, too, are unlucky, don't mourn those lost days on the beach, enjoy instead long leisurely meals, for Elban cooking has much to offer. Da Guerra in Portoferraio is a large family-run trattoria, serving excellent fish as well as other specialities.

· RISO NERO ·
Black Rice (4~6)

Riso nero was originally a Florentine dish, but it could have travelled to Elba with anyone from Cosimo de'Medici onwards. Don't be put off by its appearance ~ riso nero means black rice and black it is (made so by the cuttlefish ink-sac). But it's also a wonderful dish.

1 LB 8 OZ / 700 G SMALL CUTTLEFISH OR BABY SQUID
½ ONION, FINELY CHOPPED
3 HEAPED TBSP FINELY CHOPPED PARSLEY
2 CLOVES GARLIC, CRUSHED
1 LB 2 OZ / 500 G TOMATOES, PEELED, SEEDED AND PUT THROUGH A FOOD PROCESSOR OR VEGETABLE MILL
¼ CRUSHED CHILI PEPPER
¼ PT / 120 ML OLIVE OIL
1 LB / 450 G ITALIAN ARBORIO RICE
SEA SALT
BLACK PEPPER
½ PT / 300 ML DRY WHITE WINE

Wash the cuttlefish very well, taking care not to break the ink-sacs which should be cut off and kept aside. Chop the fish, including the tentacles, quite finely. In a deep saucepan heat the oil and cook the onion gently until soft, then add the cuttlefish. Simmer for about 10 minutes, then add the white wine. When this has evaporated put in the tomatoes, parsley, garlic, chili and salt & pepper to taste. Cook for another 15 minutes, adding water if necessary, as the sauce must be quite liquid to cook the rice. Add the rice and the 'ink' from the fish and stir well. Continue as for any other risotto: adding a little water at intervals as the rice absorbs the liquid. Once the rice is added the cooking time should be approximately 20~30 minutes. Serve hot, as a starter or light dinner.

TRIGLIA alla LIVORNESE
· Red mullet as · cooked in Livorno (4)

Livorno may not be a city that most tourists would choose to visit, but from its substantial port area come many of Tuscany's most famous fish recipes. If you encounter them far from Livorno, their heavy use of tomatoes, garlic and parsley is a clue to their origins.

12 SMALL CLEANED RED MULLETS
1 LB 2 OZ/500 G TOMATOES, PEELED, SEEDED & CHOPPED
2 CLOVES GARLIC, CRUSHED
2 SPRIGS FRESH THYME
SEA SALT
BLACK PEPPER
4 TBSP CHOPPED PARSLEY
FLOUR
OLIVE OIL FOR FRYING
½ HOT CHILI PEPPER, CRUSHED

Dust the fish liberally with flour and put in a large frying pan in which the oil has been heating. Fry for about 3~4 minutes on each side. Remove fish from pan and keep warm. Add garlic, 3 tablespoons of the parsley, thyme, and chili and cook until the garlic begins to brown. Then add tomatoes, salt and pepper and cook over a low flame for 20~30 minutes or just until the sauce begins to thicken. Return the fish to the pan, taking care not to break them and cook for a further 5 minutes. Sprinkle with remaining parsley and serve immediately.

SPECIALITA SALUMI

CASINALBO **Montorsi** (MODENA)
FRANCESCO & FIGLI

PILES OF CHEESE & SALAMI IN A PISA SHOP

One of the nicest and fastest ways to find the 'real' Pisa (not the easiest thing to do) is to wander the rabbit warren of narrow streets leading off Piazza S. Uomobuono, the main market square. Here there are vendors selling every imag~ inable, and some unimaginable, type of produce. At Tuttovo, 1 Piazza Donati, you can watch through a glass wall while they make a startling variety of pasta: everything from wild nettle ravioli to bitter chocolate tagliatelle. And there are almost as many different types and ages of Tuscan pecorino cheese at the Casa del Formaggio, where an astute enquiry may yield a free taste.

POLLO all'ARRABIATA
'Enraged' chicken (4)

This recipe is best made with the excellent free~range chickens sold at the butcher's shop in the main piazza, but is almost as good with a more ordinary bird.

1 CHICKEN, ABOUT 2½ LB/1 KG, CUT IN PIECES
1 LARGE ONION, FINELY CHOPPED
½ HOT CHILI PEPPER, SLIGHTLY CRUSHED
2 CLOVES GARLIC, CRUSHED
4~5 TOMATOES, PEELED, SEEDED AND ROUGHLY CHOPPED
½ PT/275 ML CHIANTI WINE
3 TBSP OLIVE OIL
SALT & PEPPER

Heat the oil in a large heavy saucepan and sauté the onion and garlic until golden (but not brown). Add the chicken pieces and brown well on all sides. Then add the wine, chili pepper, salt and pepper and cook over a low heat, turning frequently, until the wine is half evaporated. At this point add the tomatoes, cover and continue cooking for another 25 minutes or until the chicken is tender. Delicious when served with plain tagliatelle tossed in a little olive oil and lots of freshly chopped parsley.

* Other popular and delicious variations on this recipe are: the addition of 4 tsps of finely chopped capers (soaked in water to remove some of the vinegar) and 1 finely chopped anchovy fillet 10 minutes before the end of the cooking; the addition of two large finely sliced red or green peppers 15 minutes before the end of cooking; the addition of a generous handful of small green olives (previously rinsed in cold water) at the start of cooking the chicken pieces.

· CECI alla PISANA ·
Chickpea stew (4~6)

This is a hearty peasant stew that is even better cooked in advance, reheated and served in the same dish.

11 oz / 300 g DRIED CHICKPEAS
2 LARGE RIPE TOMATOES,
   PEELED & CHOPPED
2 TBSP FRESH CHOPPED
   ROSEMARY
4~6 SLICES OF BREAD
2 LARGE TINNED SARDINES,
   WASHED UNDER RUNNING
   WATER & MASHED
1 MEDIUM ONION, FINELY
   CHOPPED
3 CLOVES GARLIC
11 oz / 300 g BEET TOPS OR
   DARK GREEN CABBAGE
OLIVE OIL
COARSE SEA SALT
FRESHLY GROUND BLACK
   PEPPER

Cover the chickpeas with water and soak overnight in a warm place. Drain, cover with fresh water bring to boil and cook for 1½ hours or until tender. Drain, but keep the cooking liquid. Saute the onion, sardines and garlic in oil over medium heat in a heavy saucepan. Meanwhile briefly blanch the beet tops in some of the water used to cook the chickpeas. Remove the garlic (or not, as desired) from the onion and sardines and add the chickpeas, beet tops (with half a cup of their water), tomatoes, salt and pepper. Cook covered for about 3 hours on a low heat, adding several tablespoons of chickpea liquid if the stew seems to be drying out. Put a slice of grilled or toasted bread in each soup bowl, pour the stew over and serve with a jug of cold olive oil in which the rosemary has previously been heated for 10~15 minutes. A large bowl of bitter greens such as curly endive, chicory & dandelions makes a good accompaniment to this dish, especially if the greens are tossed with lemon juice and herb-flavoured olive oil.

8 SMALL NEW POTATOES
7 OZ/200 G TUNA FISH (IN
   OLIVE OIL)
1 MEDIUM RED ONION,
   SLICED PAPER THIN
2~3 TBSP WHITE
   WINE VINEGAR, TO
   TASTE
   HANDFUL FINELY
   CHOPPED PARSLEY
1 CLOVE GARLIC,
   CRUSHED
4~5 TBSP
   OLIVE OIL
   SALT & PEPPER

Boil the pot~ atoes in their skins until tender but still firm. Cut in halves or quarters dep~ ending on their size. While still warm season with garlic, oil, vinegar and onions. Break up the tuna with a fork and add to the potatoes. Sprinkle with parsley and salt and pepper to taste.

INSALATA di TONNO • e PATATE •

Tuna & potato salad (4)

The Tuscan salad of tuna and beans is not so much famous as infamous but when there are fresh white cannelloni beans available it is still a delicious summer dish. An alternative, suggested by a fishmonger in Pisa's market, is to sub~ stitute tiny new potatoes for the beans. He uses fresh tuna, barbecued over a chestnut fire, but the dish is still tasty when made with good tinned tuna

✳ TONNO e FAGIOLI

To make the classic bean salad, substitute 7 oz/200g dried white beans for potatoes. Soak the beans overnight. Rinse and boil in fresh water until tender (1~1¼ hrs). Drain and follow the recipe above. If using fresh cannelloni beans boil in water for 40 minutes. This makes a lovely summer meal when served with chilled Pappa al Pomodoro.

Sergio Lorenzi was not born a cook. Or perhaps he was just late in discovering his vocation. Although these days he is better with food, he worked first as a mechanic and still has a gruff straightforward manner that belies his rather more delicate touch in the kitchen. His lively and fashionable res~ taurant on the river Arno in Pisa is one of the best in the city, specializing in elegant versions of the local cuisine like 'Cee alla Pisana' (see page 140) and Trippa, spicy with nutmeg and fresh herbs. He serves (and sells) oil made from his own olives and swears it is some of the best in Tuscany for raw vegetables and salads because of the salty sea breezes that blow in from the coast.

ZUPPA del TARLATI VESCOVO
· Chicken soup ·
alla Bishop Tarlati (8~10)

Shortly after opening his own restaurant in 1976 Sergio wrote a cookbook with every~ thing in it from tips on how to organise a good kitchen, to recipes retrieved from rare sixteenth~century notes found in a Tuscan library. Among the recipes was this one from Arezzo for Zuppa del Tarlati Vescovo which Bishop Tarlati may well have brought with him from the papal court in Avignon. Its creamy richness bears a close resemblance to the French 'Soupe à la Reine'.

2 OZ/50 G BUTTER
2 OZ/50 G PLAIN WHITE FLOUR
3½ PT/2 LTRS GOOD CHICKEN STOCK
2½ LB/1.3 KG BOILING CHICKEN
1 ONION, COARSELY CHOPPED
1 STICK CELERY & LEAVES, COARSELY CHOPPED
½ TSP WHOLE PEPPERCORNS
3~4 CLOVES
2 BAY LEAVES
100 G DOUBLE CREAM
4 PIECES OF BREAD, CUT IN HALF & TOASTED OR FRIED IN OIL
SALT

In a heavy saucepan, melt the butter and mix in the flour to make a roux. Very slowly add the chicken stock, stirring well with a wooden spoon to avoid lumps. Bring slowly to a boil, still stirring. In the meantime wash the chicken and stuff with the onion, celery, peppercorns, cloves and bayleaves. Sew up the cavity to prevent anything escaping. Put the chicken in the broth already prepared and simmer for 45 minutes to an hour. Take the chicken out, remove skin and chop the breast meat finely. Pound the thigh meat into a paste in a mortar and mix thoroughly with the cream. Skim the original broth and add slowly to the mixture to obtain a smooth velvety soup. Stir in the breast meat, salt to taste, reheat and serve over the bread.

MINESTRA di PESCE
· Fish soup (4~6) ·

Sergio originally comes from Camaiore, between Lucca and Viareggio, an area that probably has more soup recipes per square mile than anywhere in Tuscany. This is one for a fish soup that unlike Cacciuco, is very simple to prepare. A speciality of the trawling fishermen of the river Serchio, it should, if
(continued...)

(continued...)
possible, have eel in it to make
a good traditional soup.

1½ lB/700G SALT WATER FISH
   (ANCHOVIES, BRILL ETC)
   CLEANED & CUT INTO
   LARGE CHUNKS
11 oz/300G FRESH WATER FISH (EEL,
   TROUT ETC) CLEANED & CUT
   INTO LARGE CHUNKS
3~4 CLOVES GARLIC, CRUSHED
HANDFUL ROUGHLY CHOPPED
   FRESH PARSLEY
1 ONION, CHOPPED
1 STICK CELERY, CHOPPED
1 CARROT, CHOPPED
2 TOMATOES, CHOPPED
PEEL OF 1 LEMON
RIND (LEFTOVER) OF PECORINO
   OR PARMESAN CHEESE
6 TBSP OLIVE OIL
SALT & PEPPER

In 3½ pints/1½ litres water
boil the onion, carrot, celery,
tomatoes, lemon peel and
cheese rind for about 20
minutes. In the meantime
put the oil and garlic in a
large heavy pan until the
garlic slightly browns. Add
the chopped parsley and stir
2 or 3 times, then add the
fish. Brown slightly on
both sides, then add to the
broth and continue to boil
for about 20 minutes. Ad~
just salt and pepper and
put everything through a
food processor or vegetable
mill (not too fine as the
soup should have a chunky
texture). Pour the soup into
a tureen into which you
have put 2 large slices of
bread fried in oil & rubbed
with garlic.

· SORBETTO al VINO ·
ROSSO CON PROFUMO
—— di LAMPONE ——

Red wine sorbet with
raspberries (4~6)

Like so many other excellent
ideas, the making of fresh
fruit sorbets was invented
in Tuscany, taken to France
in the sixteenth century
and made famous there.
However, it still remains a
very Italian skill. At Sergio's
a light sorbet like this one
is often served between
courses to provide a refreshing
pause, particularly between
dishes of fish and meat.

---

1 PINT/½ LTR YOUNG RED
   WINE, PREFERABLY FIZZY
7 OZ/200 G FRESH RASPBERRIES,
   SLIGHTLY CRUSHED
5 OZ/150 G SUGAR
5~6 FRESH MINT LEAVES
   (AND MORE FOR GARNISH)

Boil the sugar, mint leaves
and wine together for 2
minutes or until the sugar
is dissolved. Add to the
raspberries and allow to sit
for at least 1 hour, stirring
occasionally. Remove the
mint and put the mixture
through a food processor.
Freeze in an ice tray in the
freezer (normal ice~making
setting) for about 3 hours,
stirring frequently until
no more ice crystals form.
Serve with more mint
leaves (dipped in
sugar & water,
then frozen)
as a
garnish.

A variation on this basic red wine sorbet is to add the finely grated peel (using only the outside skin, not the white pith) of ½ an orange or ½ a lemon just before freezing. Or, for a more del~ icately coloured sorbet, use one of the new pale Tuscan rosés or spumante~style sparkling wines instead of the red wine suggested, and white seedless grapes instead of the raspberries.

Walk around the rather seedy streets of Viareggio now and it is possible to chart the gradual decline over the decades of this once grand old dame of Italian coastal resorts. Her heyday was the turn of the century when most of the still remarkably beautiful Art Nouveau hotels and casinos were built. Then came the slightly less elegant, but still sleek 1920s and 1930s, with their ocean liner façades and Art Deco neon signs. Then, finally, the inevitable 1960's and 1970's plasticized consumerism. Viareggio today is more deserving of a place in her own outrageous spring carnival than in a polite drawing room. But if the pearls are a bit tarnished, the oysters and clams are still fresh, and it is possible to find hidden in the back-streets some of the best fish restaurants in Tuscany. One is Romano Franceschini's, where he and his wife Franca, who is the cook, serve excellent versions of local seafood specialities.

SPAGHETTI al CARTOCCIO
Spaghetti with seafood cooked in a bag (4)

This is one of Franca's special recipes. When the 'cartoccio' is opened at the table it gives off a delicious aroma that is one of the highlights of the dish.

11 OZ/300 G SPAGHETTI
20 BABY SQUID, CLEANED *
4 GIANT PRAWNS
10 BABY CLAMS, CLEANED
8 LARGE CLAMS, CLEANED
6 MUSSELS, CLEANED
1 RED MULLET, CLEANED & BONED
1 CLOVE GARLIC, CRUSHED
6~8 BASIL LEAVES
6 TBSP OLIVE OIL
4 RIPE TOMATOES, PEELED,
   SEEDED & FINELY CHOPPED
1/4 CHILI PEPPER, FINELY CHOPPED
2 TBSP PARSLEY, FINELY CHOPPED
SALT

Put 5 PT/3 LTR water in a large saucepan and bring to the boil. Meanwhile heat the oil in a cast-iron pan and in it cook the chili, garlic and all the fish. After 5~10 minutes, add the tomatoes, basil and parsley. Cook over a low heat for another 5~10 minutes. When the water in the big pot is boiling add salt and the spaghetti. When half cooked, drain and add to the fish. Adjust seasoning. Take a large piece of aluminum foil and fold it in half. Open it out flat and place on a large plate or serving dish. Put the fish and spaghetti on half the foil. Fold the edges of the foil together on all three sides so no juices or steam can escape. Place the dish in an oven preheated to 475°F/250°C/Gas 9 for 5 minutes or until the foil puffs up. Take immediately to the table and serve.
* To clean clams & mussels, scrub the shells with a stiff brush under cold running water until clean. Cut off the mussels' beards (the stringy tufts that protrude from the shells) and discard any of the shellfish that are not tightly

(continued...)

· PENNE ·

· PAPPARDELLE ·

· RAVIOLI · ROLLING · PIN ·

· RAVIOLI · STAMP ·

· RAVIOLI ·

· TORTELLI ·

· TAGLIATELLE ·

· MACCHERONI ·
(TUSCAN)

· FUSILLI ·

· PICI ·

(continued from previous page...)
closed, or rather that do not close up again
when lightly tapped. Continue to rinse the
shellfish under running water until no
more sand or grit appears.

ROMBO al FORNO con ASPARAGI
• Turbot baked with asparagus (6) •

This is another of Franca Franceschini's
modern adaptations of a regional fish dish.

1 LB 12 OZ / 800 G TURBOT
6 SCAMPI
1 OZ / 20 G BUTTER
2 TBSP OIL
20 ASPARAGUS TIPS
2 WINE GLASSES FISH STOCK
SALT & PEPPER

Clean & wash the turbot. Shell the scampi
& remove the black intestinal track but not
the heads. Pat fish dry and flour lightly,
only flouring the

white part of the turbot. Arrange the fish in a greased baking dish with the asparagus tips, salt & freshly ground black pepper. Dot with butter and pour over the oil & about 2 wine glasses of good fish stock. Bake in an oven preheated to 400°F/200°C/Gas 6 for 20 minutes. Serve hot.

✻Make good fish stock by boiling together the following ingredients: 4 or 5 fish heads, ½ onion, 1 bay leaf, 1 stick celery, 5 peppercorns, 1 tsp sea salt. 1 clove garlic, 5 wine glasses water & 5 tbsp dry white wine. After 20 minutes, remove the bay leaf & pass other ingredients through a food processor or mouli.

MARTINELLI

MARTINELLI

UMBRELLA CASES
OFF SEASON
-VIAREGGIO.

· THE CERRAGIOLI FAMILY ·

Drive up into the hills between Camaiore and Lucca and keep going until you run out of road. If you have taken the right road you will probably be at the village of Greppolungo. Park your car and walk to the only alimentari shop there. You will find Paulo Cerragioli and his wife selling their own excellent olive oil and, if you are lucky and have had the sense to ring beforehand, they will be ready and willing to cook you an excellent meal. They serve only a few dishes, and theirs is the real 'casalinga' ~ the home cooking that is almost impossible to find in restaurants.

LA GALLINA RIPIENA
Stuffed chicken (6)

This recipe for stuffed boiled chicken is one of the best and most typical of the Camaiore area. At Greppolungo they splash rough red wine into the chicken broth just before serving, an interesting Tuscan variation on sherry in consomme.

1 LARGE BOILING FOWL WITH
    GIBLETS
2 CARROTS
1 STICK CELERY
1 ONION
SALT
1 LEEK
OLIVE OIL

FOR THE STUFFING
2 SLICES HAM OR MORTADELLA
    SAUSAGE, CHOPPED
2 SPRIGS FRESH THYME, CHOPPED
3 SLICES BREAD, SOAKED IN MILK
6 TBSP PECORINO CHEESE, GRATED
8 OZ/225 G GROUND (MINCED) VEAL
    OR LEAN BEEF
1 ~ 2 EGGS
2 CLOVES GARLIC, CRUSHED
4 TBSP OLIVE OIL
3 TBSP PARSLEY, FINELY CHOPPED
1/2 ~ 3/4 TSP NUTMEG

First make the stuffing. In a large frying pan gently cook the chicken giblets in the oil until they change colour. Chop finely and reserve. Add the sausage, meat and garlic to the pan and cook just until the meat starts to brown. Mix with the giblets, herbs, bread, cheese and 1 beaten egg. If this does not bind the stuffing, add another beaten egg.

Clean, wash and dry the inside of the chicken. Pack loosely with the stuffing ~ the stuffing tends to swell in cooking and you don't want an exploding chicken. Sew up both ends of the chicken so that nothing can escape. Put in a large flame-proof casserole with the carrots, celery, onion, leek and salt and cover with water. The water should be about 1in/2.5cm over the chicken. Bring to a boil and then simmer over a low heat for about 2 1/2 hours, until the chicken is cooked. Remove it from the pan, cut the threads, carefully lift out the stuffing, which should be quite solid, and serve both the chicken and the stuffing sliced thinly and garnished with either fresh thyme or Tuscan salsa verde (see page 75). To make a complete meal of this, remove the vegetables from the broth and boil fresh tortellini or ravioli gnudi (page 78) in it to serve as soup before the chicken.

Of course Caccuicco is a Mediterranean fish soup, originally from Livorno, as the Livornese will proudly tell you; and the cooks in Viareggio will disdainfully say that no good ever came from Livorno, and certainly not Caccuicco. Its a subject for endless, inconclusive debates. Certainly one of the best versions of caccuicco must be that served at the Ponte di Sasso restaurant outside Camaiore. A good caccuicco is a joy to behold, like fine wine first enjoy its rich colour, then its bouquet and finally the time the rich flavour remains on the tongue.

· CACCIUCCO ·
Fish soup (6)

Caccuicco is a poor man's dish, at least theoretically, so most of the fish should be cheap, salt water scaled ones ~ not salmon or sole! There should also be at least five different types of fish, preferably more. Franco, the brilliant chef at Ponte di Sasso, used twelve.

10 LB 10 OZ/5 KG ~½ ORDINARY SCALED FISH SUCH AS DOGFISH, NON BONY PIECES OF EEL, ½ A MIXTURE OF SQUID, CUTTLEFISH, OCTOPUS, SHRIMP, CLAMS AND MUSSELS
3 CLOVES GARLIC, CRUSHED
4 TBSP TOMATO PUREE
2 TBSP RED WINE VINEGAR
4 TBSP FRESH PARSLEY, CHOPPED
SMALL HOT CHILI PEPPERS (1~2)
½ BOTTLE ROBUST RED WINE (DRY)
6 PIECES WHOLEMEAL BREAD
2~3 TOMATOES, PEELED AND CHOPPED ROUGHLY
COARSE SEA SALT
BLACK PEPPER, FRESHLY GROUND
OLIVE OIL

Clean and scale the fish, cut off and save the heads and tails for stock. Remove the beak and insides of the squid and the cuttlefish's ink sac. (Your fishmonger may do this for you if you ask, but be sure that you ask him for the heads and tails.) Put the fish heads and tails, 1 clove garlic, 2 tbsp parsley, the tomatoes and tomato puree in a large pan with 1 pint/600 ml of water and bring to the boil. Cover and simmer for 20 minutes.

136

Discard the fish heads and tails.
Add the fish, beginning with
the boniest variety (ask your
fishmonger's advice), cover and
simmer for 20 minutes. Rub
through a sieve and continue
cooking the various more
tender fish, for a further 15
minutes. Meanwhile, saute the
other two crushed cloves
of garlic in a large
pan. When
just turning
brown
add salt,
chili pepper, pepper and remaining
parsley. Put in the shellfish, squid
and cuttlefish and when the
water they release has evap~
orated, add the vinegar. Swirl
around the pan and pour in the
red wine. When this has
almost evaporated add the extra
tomatoes (if desired) and continue
cooking for 15 minutes. Toast
the bread, rub thoroughly
with fresh garlic and put in
bowls. Pour the rest of the
fish, in their rich tomato sauce,
over the top. Serve immediately.
Cacciucco is meant to be a com~
plete meal in a dish rather
than just a first course. It
should be served with plenty
of crusty bread and look more
like a hearty fish stew than a
soup, its wide variety of fish and
crustaceans only just covered by
a thick binding of hot and gar~
licky sauce.

· POLENTA MATUFFI ·
Sausage & polenta stew (6)

This is a sturdy, old~fashioned
peasant dish, redolent of cheese
and spicy sausages. It should
be eaten with a spoon and a
minimum of good table manners,
and of course plenty of equally
(continued...)

In Viareggio there is a trad~
ition that in addition to
the healthy quantity of
whiting, hake, red mullet,
John Dory, gurnard and craw~
fish, a good cacciucco should
always contain one stone from
the ocean. Perhaps
this is because
cacciucco is a dish
that was eaten
originally only by
Tuscan fishermen. What~
ever they scooped up with
their nets and lines went in
the cooking pot.
   Although the origins
of cacciucco are thus very
humble, it can be made
as elegant as the fish
used. The only absolutely
essential ingredient
(apart from the stone) is
the hot chili pepper.

(continued from previous page,
sturdy young red wine should be
available to wash it down.

1 LB 2 OZ/500 G FINE GRAIN CORN
    MEAL, SIFTED
6 BIG LEAN TUSCAN SAUSAGES
1/4 PT/120 ML OLIVE OIL
2 LB 2 OZ/1 KG TOMATOES, PEELED
    AND CHOPPED
3/4 OZ/15 G DRIED MUSHROOMS,
    SOAKED FOR AT LEAST 10 MINUTES
    IN WARM WATER, DRAINED
    & CHOPPED
1 SMALL CARROT, CHOPPED
1 SMALL STICK CELERY, CHOPPED
1 ONION, CHOPPED
BAY LEAF
1/2 BOTTLE RED WINE
GENEROUS QUANTITIES OF
    GRATED PECORINO OR PARMESAN
SALT & PEPPER

Heat the oil in a medium-sized
saucepan. Saute the carrot,
onion and celery in it until
softened. Mash the sausages
with a fork, add to the pan and
brown with the vegetables. Skim
off 1/2 the fat (if there is any) and
add the red wine. When it has
almost evaporated add the mushrooms. Brown and put in the
tomatoes and bay leaf. Simmer
gently for 20 minutes. Meanwhile bring 1 3/4 pt/1 ltr of
salted water to the boil in a
large pan. Add the corn meal
very slowly, stirring constantly
with a wooden spoon to prevent
lumps forming. Continue
cooking and stirring for 20
minutes. Then put a ladleful
of polenta into each bowl,
followed by a ladleful of sauce &
lots of cheese. Continue in
layers with each bowl until the
sauce is finished.

Scarpaccia is a zucchini pie without pastry from the region around Camaiore. At the beautiful Art Nouveau hotel Il Giardinetto in northern Tuscany they serve a delicious version called Torta di Zucchini, as well as another delicious Tuscan side dish, Panzerotti. These are golf~ball size pieces of raw bread dough that are wrapped around chunks of cooked sausage or pecorino cheese and then deep~fried to a crisp gol~ den brown and sprinkled with coarse sea~salt.

SCARPACCIA
Zucchini pie (6)

The name Scarpaccia means 'old, flat battered shoe' and refers to the fact that the pie should have a sim~ ilar appearance. There are two versions, a sweet one somewhat like Lucca's Torta di Verdure (page 148) and this savoury one, an ideal side dish with summer roasts and salads.

14 OZ /400G SMALLEST ZUCCHINI/
  COURGETTES (WITH THEIR
  FLOWERS IF POSSIBLE)
3 LARGE SPRING ONIONS, FINELY
  CHOPPED
½ CLOVE GARLIC, CRUSHED
½ CUP MILK & WATER, MIXED
4 TBSP FLOUR, SIFTED
2 EGGS
4 TBSP GRATED PARMESAN
SALT & PEPPER
OLIVE OIL

Finely chop the zucchini. Salt them and allow to drain for 20 minutes. In the meantime, beat together the eggs, flour, milk and water to form a smooth batter. Rinse salt off the zucchini and dry with kitchen paper towels. Mix the zucchini, onions, cheese and garlic into the batter and pour into 2 greased 8in/ 20.5 cm baking tins. (You can use 1 large one, but the batter should not be more than ½ in /1 cm deep.) Drizzle sev~ eral tablespoons of olive oil on top and bake in an oven pre~ heated to 425°F/220°C/Gas 7 until set and golden brown on top ~ about 30 minutes. Serve with more grated cheese on top if desired.

· CEE alla PISANA ·

Probably the most famous dish in Pisa
is 'Cee alla Pisana'. Cee is Tuscan
slang for 'cieche' meaning blind, and
also for the tiny baby eels ('elvers' in England)
that are caught at the mouth of the Arno
during the winter months. In Pisa the
eels (4 oz/100g per person), are first
washed several times and dried very well.
Then they are put into a frying pan with
lots of very hot oil in which have been
browned 2 cloves of garlic, 3~4 sage leaves
and ½ hot chili pepper finely chopped. The
little eels, no more than 3 in/7.5 cm long, are
stirred rapidly for about 15 minutes until
they turn white, then mixed with 2 beaten
eggs, the juice of
a lemon and 3
tablespoons grated
parmesan. This is
stirred until just
barely set and
served still creamy,
looking rather like
spaghetti carbonara.

OLIVES & CHESTNUTS

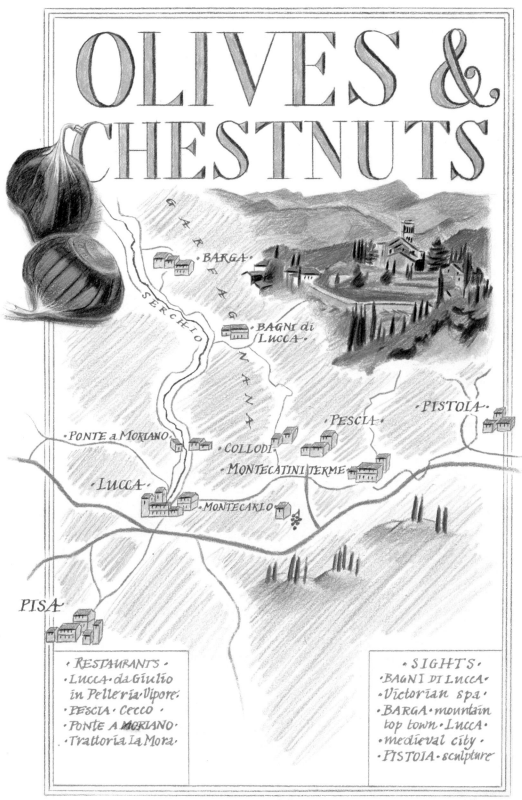

GARFAGNANA

SERCHIO

• BARGA •

• BAGNI di LUCCA •

• PISTOIA •

• PESCIA •

• PONTE a MORIANO •

• COLLODI •

• MONTECATINI TERME •

• LUCCA •

• MONTECARLO •

PISA •

• RESTAURANTS •
• LUCCA • da Giulio
in Pelleria • Vipore •
• PESCIA • Cecco •
• PONTE A MORIANO •
• Trattoria La Mora •

• SIGHTS •
• BAGNI DI LUCCA •
• Victorian spa •
• BARGA • mountain
top town • LUCCA •
• medieval city •
• PISTOIA • sculpture

· INTRODUCTION ·

The Garfagnana and Pistoian mountains, high foot-hills of the rugged Appennines, are divided lengthwise by the river Serchio. Tiny villages, where rocks hold red roof tiles in place, cling perilously to steep hillsides, their bars and outdoor cafes dropping away to the valleys below. Because this is a relatively poor region of Tuscany, the best cooking makes good use of available local products ~ trout fresh from the rivers, porcini the size of t-bone steaks and a stunning variety of other wild mushrooms, simple flat cakes made with sweet chestnut flour and smeared with honey and creamy ricotta cheese, and everywhere near Lucca, the famous Luccan olive oil, considered the best in the world.

Perhaps because of its remoteness and its history of poverty, the wild Garfagnana region north of Lucca remains unspoilt, in fact almost undiscovered, by the tourists that have overrun the Tuscan coast. Hill towns like beautiful Barga, with steep cobbled streets and honey~coloured buildings, have sweeping views of pine forests, castles and distant snowy mountains. West of Barga, straggling along rivers a startling shade of turquoise, are towns whose streets rise almost vertically from the river bank into high mountain fields. During World War 2 many of these moun~tain villages were havens for the Italian resistance, their remoteness making them almost impossible for the government troops to control. Memories of those war years are still fresh and many stories are told in the bars of escaped prisoners hidden for months in cellars or shepherds' huts.

On the southernmost edge of the Garfagnana moun~tains lies walled Lucca, birthplace of the opera composer Giacomo Puccini, and the only city in Tuscany to resist Florence successfully. It remained an indep~endant city state until becoming part of the Grand Duchy of Tuscany in the nineteenth century and even today preserves an air of aloofness.

Lucca, with Siena, is one of the loveliest small cities in Italy. The poverty of the Garfagnana seems not to have penetrated the massive sixteenth century walls. John Ruskin, writing in the nineteenth

century, claimed to have begun his study of architecture af~
ter seeing Lucca's beautifully preserved twelfth~century
buildings, built '... in material so incorruptible, that
after 600 years of sunshine & rain, a lancet could not now
be put between their joints.' Narrow medieval streets
between these buildings lead quietly to huge windy piazzas
and past elaborate Romanesque churches like tiered
marble wedding cakes.

From the plane tree~shaded pathway that tops the city
walls living trees growing on the high tower of the
Palazzo Guinigi are clearly visible, as are private and
public gardens hidden from city streets by the red
brick facades of palaces built during the fourteenth
and fifteenth centuries~Lucca's richest period. The
Palazzo Pfanner is one of the most elegant with symmet~
rical rows of white marble statues and lemon trees in
terracotta pots, but it cannot match for splendour the
summer palaces outside Lucca, built by Lucchese
nobility between the sixteenth and eighteenth centuries.
Three of them, Villa Imperiale at Marlia, Villa Mansi at Seg~
romigno & Villa Torrigiani at Camigliano, lie in magnificent
gardens in cool hills to the north of the city. At the Villa Imp~
eriale, summer residence of Napoleon's sister Elisa Baciocchi,
Paganini (said to have been one of her many lovers) gave his first
musical performance.

It is not only Lucca's past that is attractive. Like Siena
the city is famous for its sweet breads and pastries,
and where better to sample them than sitting in one of
the many sunny cafés, set in flowered courtyards, dis~
tracted only by the
occasional (and in~
evitable) moped
buzzing past?

· P A L A Z Z O · P F A N N E R ·

144

· L U C C A ·

Lucca is an elegant little city rather than a town and the pleasures to be enjoyed there are naturally rather more sophisticated than in the villages of the Garfagnana. The lovely, well~preserved turn~of~the~century shop fronts and signs are particularly pleasing. If you're exploring the city walls on a hot day, a glass of the local white wine, Montecarlo Buonamico, at the beautiful Antico Caffè della Mura, is a certain reviver. Or, in less auspicious weather, find your way to Puccini's favourite cafe, Cafe di Simo, for cups of frothy cappucino and Torta di Verdure, Lucca's great speciality.

· TORTA di VERDURE ·
Sweet spinach pie

This sweet is sold in most of Lucca's delicatessans & tastes something like a Tuscan ver~ sion of American pumpkin pie.

FOR THE PASTRY
11 oz/300g PLAIN WHITE FLOUR
3¼ oz/80g SUGAR
4 oz/100g BUTTER, SOFTENED
2 EGG YOLKS
PINCH SALT

FOR THE FILLING
7 oz/200g ZUCCHINI/COURGETTES
11 oz/300g SPINACH OR
  SWISS CHARD
3 oz/75g SUGAR
2 oz/50g PINE NUTS
1¼ oz/30g RAISINS
1 EGG, BEATEN
2 TBSP GRATED ORANGE PEEL
2 TBSP GRATED PARMESAN
½ TSP CINNAMON
½ TSP NUTMEG
PINCH SALT
1~1¼ oz/25~30g BUTTER

To make the pastry, sift the flour on to a pastry board or work~ surface. Make a hole in the middle and put in the butter, sugar, salt and egg yolks. Work into a soft smooth dough with your fingertips. Cover and leave for 2 hours in a warm place.

To make the filling, first chop the zucchini and spinach finely, discarding any tough stalks. Wash and drain well, then sim~ mer in the butter until soft. Let cool and then mix well with the other ingredients.

When the dough is ready, cut off about a quarter and keep aside to make a lattice top for the pie. Roll the remainder out into a large circle and place in a greased, floured flan dish. Pour in the filling. Roll out the remaining pastry and cut into strips for the lattice top. Brush with beaten egg yolk and bake for 25~30 minutes in an oven preheated to 375°F/190°C/Gas 5 (until a toothpick put into the centre of the pie comes out dry).

145

Lucca and olives are synonymous. In fact some gastronomes consider the delicate Luccan olive oils to be among the world's best, although there is stiff competition from i colli senesi oils ~ the green gold of the hills around Siena. When the olives are plump and ideal for eating, they are pickled with lemon, cinnamon, salt and hot chili peppers ~a par~ ticular speciality at the Ristorante Vipore, west of Lucca. Or else they are used to add bite to fatty rabbit or lamb stews, as in the recipe below.

AGNELLO con OLIVE NERE
Lamb and black olive stew (4~6)

Variations on this recipe are served in many of the restaur~ ants of the area, but it is par~ ticularly good at the Buca di San Antonio as well as at the little cafe Da Giulio, both in the back streets of Lucca.

You can give this dish some~ thing of the tang provided by fresh olives if you add a table~ spoon of grated lemon peel during the cooking.

2 LB 2 OZ/1 KG STEWING LAMB
14-OZ /400G RIPE TOMATOES, PEELD & SEEDED
30 PLUMP BLACK OLIVES (OR MORE ACCORDING TO TASTE)
6~8 TBSP OLIVE OIL
2 SPRIGS FRESH ROSEMARY
2 (GENEROUS) WINE GLASSES OF DRY WHITE WINE
2 CLOVES GARLIC, CRUSHED
SEA SALT
BLACK PEPPER

OLIO 7500

OLIO EXTRA VERGINE DI OLIVA LUCCA

146

Put the oil in a big frying pan and gently cook the garlic and rosemary. When the garlic is golden add the lamb cut in bite size chunks and brown it. Add the wine and when it has almost evaporated, the tomatoes (and the lemon peel if desired). Stir, cover and cook over a low heat for 15 minutes. If using fresh olives boil them for several minutes; if using pickled ones (tinned, bottled etc) rinse them well. Add to the lamb, cover and cook very slowly until the meat is tender, about 1½ hours, adding warm water or stock if the stew seems to be drying out. For a less rich stew skim off any visible fat that rises during cooking. Serve poured over polenta or with tiny boiled potatoes to soak up the sauce.

✳ When buying olive oil, be sure to get 'cold pressed extra virgin' from the first pressing. It is the best, expensive even in Italy, but well worth the price. Olive oils are classed by their acidity level; the less acidic they are, the better and more costly. During oil~pressing time (Nov~Feb) around Lucca you may come across a soup called 'Zuppa alla Frantoiana' or 'oil~press soup'. It is basically a form of Ribollita. Where Ribollita is usually yesterday's minestrone re~heated today, Zuppa alla Frantoiana has zucchini, carrots, celery, onions and cabbage cooked freshly, mixed with pre~cooked beans & ham, & served with a jug of the newly pressed olive oil.

some of
'La Cucina
Povera'~
dishes
that
might
have otherwise
disappeared,
if not from Tuscan
homes, at least
from Tuscan restaur~
ant menus.

TRATTORIA LA MORA

Some restaurants serve food. Others serve atmos~ phere~a taste of a place, of its people, its countryside and its history. Sauro Brun~ icardi's Trattoria La Mora, north of Lucca, is one of these. The wine (from his own enoteca) is excel~ lent, the food delicious and creative, but almost more important is the warmth & generosity of Signor Brunicardi and his staff. Sauro Brunicardi is one of the small group of Italian restauranteurs who in 1980 formed 'La Linea Italia in Cucina' to pre~ serve the traditional reg~ ional cooking of Italy, and to serve carefully researched and prepared dishes from their own areas. As a result of this fidelity to tradition, with additional ingenuity because not all traditional food is necessarily good, it is still possible to find

· GRAN FARRO ·
Grain and bean soup (4)

Gran Farro is traditional wheat soup made in Tuscany from raw spelt (hard wheat) but if unavailable you can make a similar soup using buckwheat (kasha) boiled for about an hour.

5 OZ/150 G RAW SPELT OR
    GERMAN WHEAT, BOILED
    FOR AT LEAST 3 HOURS
9 OZ/250 G DRIED OR 1 LB 6 OZ/
    600 G FRESH KIDNEY BEANS
½ ONION, SLICED THINLY
3 TBSP OLIVE OIL
STICK CELERY, DICED WITH LEAVES
CLOVE GARLIC, CRUSHED
4 OZ/100 G PROSCIUTTO OR FATTY
    HAM, FINELY CHOPPED
8 OZ/225 G TOMATOES, PEELED,
    SEEDED & FINELY SIEVED
3~4 SAGE LEAVES
1 TSP MARJORAM
½ TSP NUTMEG
SALT &
PEPPER

Boil fresh beans in water un~
til tender (about 1~1½ hrs).
If using dried beans, soak them
overnight, rinse and then boil
in fresh water for about 45
minutes. Drain and put
through a food processor or
mouli, reserving the water &
¼ of the whole beans. Heat
the oil in a deep saucepan &
add the onion, ham, celery,
garlic, sage, marjoram and
nutmeg. Saute gently and
when the onion starts to
brown, add the tomatoes,
salt and pepper to taste. Sim~
mer for about 15 minutes
until the mixture is well
blended. Add the bean purée
with a little of its own water.
Mix well before adding the
wheat. Simmer for about 40
minutes, adding more
bean water if the soup
seems to be drying out.
About 10 minutes before
the end of this time,
add the whole beans
and allow to heat
through. Serve with a jug
of olive oil to pour over.

GARMUGIA alla LUCCHESE
· Spring vegetable ·
soup as made in Lucca (6)

This is a soup made only in
the spring when the tiniest
fresh vegetables are available.
The cooking times given are
approximate ~ the vegetables
should be just barely cooked
and served while
they are still a
bright clear green.

---

4 SPRING ONIONS,
  FINELY CHOPPED
1LB 2oz/500G GROUND
  (MINCED) LEAN BEEF
4 oz/100G PROSCIUTTO OR BACON
7oz/200G FRESH BROAD BEANS,
  SHELLED
TENDER LEAVES FROM 3 ART~
  ICHOKES, TRIMMED
9oz/250G FRESH
  PEAS, SHELLED
2 CLOVES GARLIC
7oz/200G TENDER
  ASPARAGUS, CHOPPED
3~4 CUPS BEEF STOCK
5 TBSP OLIVE OIL
SALT & PEPPER

Heat the oil in a deep pan. Add
the onions, garlic & ham &
when the onion starts to brown
add the beef. Saute for 5 min~
utes, then add the artichokes
and broad beans. If the mix~
ture needs moistening, add
a drop or two of oil, but if pos~
sible the vegetables should cook
in their own juices. When the
vegetables are starting to soften,
but still firm, pour in the stock.
After 5~10 minutes, add peas &
asparagus & cook until tender.
Serve over toasted bread.

· CRESPELLE ·
alla FIORENTINA
Spinach crepes

This dish is of questionable
Tuscan origin, but Beppe the
chef makes crepes with such
verve and expertise it would
be a pity to leave them out.
You can toss the pancakes if
you do not possess the asbes~
tos fingertips needed to
turn them by hand as
Beppe does.

· FOR THE BATTER ·
3½ OZ / 90 G PLAIN WHITE FLOUR
3 EGGS, BEATEN
2 WINEGLASSES MILK
SALT
OIL

· FOR THE FILLING ·
14 OZ / 400 G RICOTTA
1 LB 6 OZ / 600 G FRESH SPINACH
1 EGG, BEATEN
½ TSP NUTMEG
SALT
FRESHLY GROUND BLACK
    PEPPER

· FOR THE SAUCE ·

3 OZ/75G FLOUR PLAIN WHITE

3 OZ/75 G BUTTER

1¼ PT/¾ LTR MILK

SALT & PEPPER

5 TBSP OF A HOMEMADE TOMATO SAUCE (AS A GARNISH) OR 3 VERY TASTY TOMATOES, PEELED, SEEDED & FINELY CHOPPED

3 TBSP GRATED PECORINO OR PARMESAN CHEESE

To make the filling, trim & clean spinach, remove any tough stalks and cook, covered, in a little water until tender. Drain well through a fine~mesh sieve or strainer, pressing with the back of a wooden spoon to get out all the water. Chop very finely and mix with the other ingredients.

To make the sauce, melt the butter in a pan, add the flour and once blended with the fat, cook for a few minutes over a low heat. Add the milk gradually, stirring all the time to prevent lumps forming. When all the milk has been added, raise the temperature and bring sauce to the boil. Cook for 2~3 minutes, continuing to stir. Remove from the heat and add salt and black pepper to taste.

To make the crepes, sift the flour into a basin, make a well in the middle and put in the eggs and salt. Beat in the milk gradually, using either a wooden spatula or a small sauce whisk. Stir rapidly at first, then more slowly while mixing the flour from the sides of the bowl. The batter must be quite liquid and never thick or doughy. Leave for 30 minutes. Heat a crepe pan or else a smooth frying pan with round sides and when very hot wipe with a cloth or pastry brush dipped in oil. Immediately ladle or pour in just enough batter to make a paper thin covering over the bottom of the pan ~ swirl the batter around the pan as you pour because it will set quickly. When bubbles form and the edges curl away from the sides of the pan, gently lift the pancake with your fingertips or a spatula and flip it over to cook the other side. Continue with the rest of the batter. Spread each pancake with some of the stuffing, roll up and put in a greased baking dish. Cover with the sauce, the tomatoes and the grated cheese. Bake in an oven preheated to 350°F/180°C/Gas 4 for 15~20 minutes and then under a grill for a minute or two to make the top bubbling and golden. Serve with a crisp salad as a starter or light main course.

Driving to the Eremo di Cal~omini it is increasingly clear why it is obligat~ory to sound the car horn. A nar~row mountain road with snake~like bends and recent worrying evidence of landslides leads slowly but per~sistently upwards to the final breath~taking view from this isolated monas~tery, that at weekends has an open-air restaurant. It serves some of the best trout in Tuscany ~ if not the world ~ caught in the stream running beside the restaurant.

TROTA alla GARFAGNANA

Grilled trout as cooked in the Garfagnana

1 TROUT PER PERSON
COARSE SEA SALT
BLACK PEPPER
LEMON JUICE
FRESH ROSEMARY
OLIVE OIL

First prepare the fire. In Tus~cany they use chestnut wood which gives a characteristic sweet taste to the fish. Failing this use a charcoal grill or the grill of your cooker. Clean, scale and rinse the trout under cold running water. Sprinkle the inside cavity with coarse sea salt, pepper and lemon juice and stuff with plenty of fresh rosemary (or if necessary use dried). Brush olive oil all ov~er the fish & on the grill rack to prev~ent sticking. Cook the fish about 4~5 in/ 10~12.5 cm from the wood or charcoal, turning only once. The fish is cooked when the juices run out clear and the flesh is opaque, about 10 minutes for a 2 lb/450 g fish. This is very good served with a simple salad of finely sliced tomatoes, red peppers and onions.

For a more substantial meal cook small potatoes and tom~atoes together as they do in the Garfagnana. Take 1~2 potatoes per person (cut in pieces if they are large) & 1 tomato, peeled & chopped for each potato. Put in a lidded flameproof casserole with 5~6 tbsp of olive oil per 6 small potatoes, 1~2 cloves of garlic, crushed, 1 carrot, 1 stick of celery and 1 large onion, all finely chopped. Add salt and black pepper to taste and cook over a low flame until the juice from the tomatoes has evaporated & potatoes are tender.

Ricotta Puna
£460

A particularly soft sweet flour is made from the chestnuts that grow so abundantly in the mountains north of the city of Pistoia. From it the local cooks make a strange, aromatic flat cake called castagnaccio. It is an acquired taste ~ difficult for non-Italians unused to sweets made with olive oil and rosemary, but certainly a taste that is very reminiscent of Tuscany.

CASTAGNACCIO
· Chestnut cake ·

This recipe comes from the big alimentari shop in Pistoia's permanent central market. The buxom proprietress was quite clearly amused that a foreigner should be asking for 'farina di castagna', chestnut flour, out of season (as the flour doesn't keep well it is only available from late autumn to spring, after the chestnut harvest) & also clearly concerned that it should be used properly.

1LB 4OZ/550G SIFTED
   CHESTNUT FLOUR
1 PT/550 ML WATER
4~5 SPRIGS ROSEMARY,
   COARSELY CHOPPED
5 TBSP OLIVE OIL
GENEROUS HANDFUL RAISINS
2½ OZ/60G PINENUTS
PINCH SALT
2 TBSP GRANULATED SUGAR

Mix chestnut flour and water carefully with wooden spoon or spatula so as not to form lumps. It should be quite a liquid batter. Add raisins, pinenuts, salt and sugar. Pour into a greased baking tray not more than 3/4 inch cm deep. Sprinkle with the rosemary and drizzle the oil over the top. Bake in an oven preheated to 400°F/200°C/Gas 6 until brown and, as the Pistoian lady described it, 'cracked like dry earth' or, more accurately, about 40 minutes. It is delicious straight from the pan either hot or cold, dredged with icing sugar or smeared with honey and fresh ricotta cheese.

• PISTOIA • EARLY MORNING MARKET •

· CECCO ·

The town of Pescia is famous for its flowers, its proximity to Pinocchio's home town of Collodi and its local Asparagi giganti, although to those of us used to small tasty green stalks, these giants of the asparagus world are not so impressive.

· ZUPPA di FUNGHI ·
Wild mushroom soup (4)

This delicious and delicate soup is made at Cecco's with an amazing quantity of fresh porcini mushrooms (BOLETUS EDULIS).

Commercial mushrooms are no substitute but you can use other wild mushrooms such as morels and chanterelles or, and only if pressed, use cultivated mush~ rooms and add ¾ oz/15g of packaged dried porcini.

1 LB/450 G SMALL CLEAN PORCINI
 (OR MORE IF YOU CAN AFFORD IT)
3~4 CUPS GOOD BEEF STOCK
CLOVE GARLIC, CRUSHED
2 TBSP PARSLEY, FINELY CHOPPED
5~6 LEAVES NEPITELLA (THIS IS
 CATMINT, IF IT IS NOT AVAILABLE
 USE ANY FRESH GARDEN MINT)
4 SLICES BREAD
OLIVE OIL
SALT & PEPPER

Heat a little olive oil in a med~ ium-sized saucepan, cut the porcini into small pieces & sauté gently with the nepitella, adding salt and pepper to taste. When browned add the stock and then simmer for 10~15 minutes (with the dried mushrooms if using). After about 7 minutes stir in the garlic and parsley pounded together in a mortar. Toast the bread and rub with a garlic clove, freshly cut. Put the bread in bowls and pour the soup over.

POLLASTRINO al MATTONE
· Chicken under a brick (2) ·

A mattone is a terracotta housebrick and the chicken in this recipe gets its character~ istic crispy texture from the weight of a heavy glazed terra~ cotta plate pressed down on it all through the cooking. You can buy traditional mattone plates in Lucca, or use any clean, heavy glazed terracotta brick.

1 SMALL CHICKEN, CUT IN HALF
 DOWN THE BREASTBONE AND
 POUNDED FAIRLY FLAT
JUICE OF 1 LEMON
CLOVE GARLIC, CRUSHED
FRESH ROSEMARY
3~4 TBSP OLIVE OIL
COARSE SEA SALT
COARSE GROUND BLACK PEPPER

Rub all the ingredients well into the chicken's skin and then put the chicken in a frying pan. Place the brick on top and fry (in plenty of olive oil) over a low heat for about 20 minutes on each side until the skin is crunchy. Or put the chicken in a mar~ inade made of the same ingredients. Leave for several hours, turning occas~ ionally, and then fry as above.

·· RESTAURANTS ··

Restaurants mentioned in
the text

·THE VALE of FLORENCE·
BORGO ANTICO ~ Piazza Santa
Spirito, Florence
LA CARABACCIA ~ Via Palazzuolo,
Florence
LE CAVE DI MAIANO ~ Via delle
Cave 16, Maiano
CIBREO ~ Via de' Macci 118/R,
Florence
COCOLEZZONE ~ Via del Parioncino,
26r, Florence
DA GANINO ~ Piazza de' Cimatori,
4, Florence
MASHA INNOCENTI (cookery
school) ~ Via Trieste 1, Florence
SOSTANZA ~ Via del Porcellana 25,
Florence

·THE CHIANTI HILLS·
ALBERGO LOCANDA GIOVANNI
DA VERRAZZANO ~ Greve
CASTELLO DI SPALTENNA ~ Gaiole
IL FEDINO ~ San Casciano in
Val di Pesa
TRATTORIA DEL MONTAGLIARI~
near Panzano

·MEDIEVAL CITIES·
BUCA DI SAN FRANCESCO ~ Via di
San Francesco 1, Arezzo
LOCANDA DELL'AMOROSA ~ Sinalunga
PONTE A RONDOLINO ~ Via Sevestro
32, San Gimignano

·VINES & VINEYARDS·
LA CASANOVA ~ Strada della
Vittoria 10, Chianciano Terme

DIVA ~ Via Gracciano nel Corso
92, Montepulciano
FATTORIA DEI BARBI ~ 4 Km
from Montalcino on the road
to Castelnuovo dell'Abate
FATTORIA LA CHIUSA ~ Via della
Madonnina 88, Montefollónico
FATTORIA PULCINO ~ Località
Fonte Castagno, Montepulciano

·THE ETRUSCAN MAREMMA·
BAR LUPI ~ Sorano
DA LAUDOMIA ~ Poderi di
Montemerano
TANA DEL CINGHIALE ~ Tirli

· BY THE SEA ·
DA GUERRA ~ Portoferraio, Elba
RENDEZ-VOUS DA MARCELLO ~
Marciana Marina, Elba
RISTORANTE ENOTECA SERGIO ~
Lungarno Pacinotti 1, Pisa
PONTE DI SASSO ~ Località Ponte
di Sasso, Viareggio
DA ROMANO ~ Via Mazzini 122,
Viareggio

· OLIVES & CHESTNUTS ·
LA BUCA DI SANT'ANTONIO, Via
della Cervia 3, Lucca
CECCO ~ Viale Forti 84, Pescia
DA GIULIO IN PELLERIA ~ via
San Tommaso 29, Lucca
TRATTORIA LA MORA ~ Località
Sesto di Moriano 104
VIPORE ~ Località Pieve Santo
Stefano

· INDEX ·

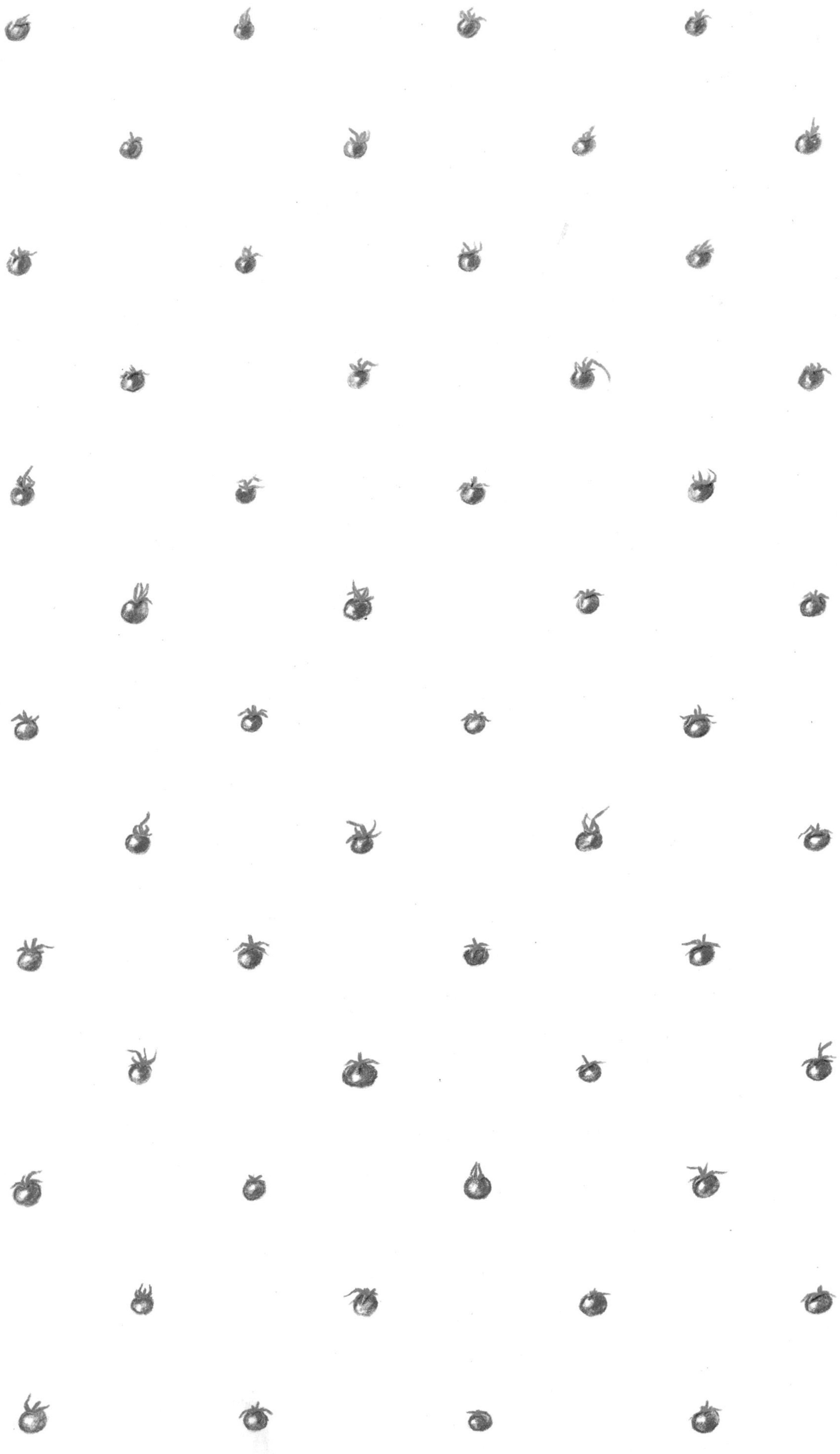